Progressive Cello Solos

Beginning Level

Christine Watts

PIANO ACCOMPANIMENTS

Piano Compositions by

Craig Levesque
Michi Tashjian
Sarah Dubois

I0808776

WWW.MELBAY.COM

Table of Contents

The Bee

German Folk Song
Craig Levesque

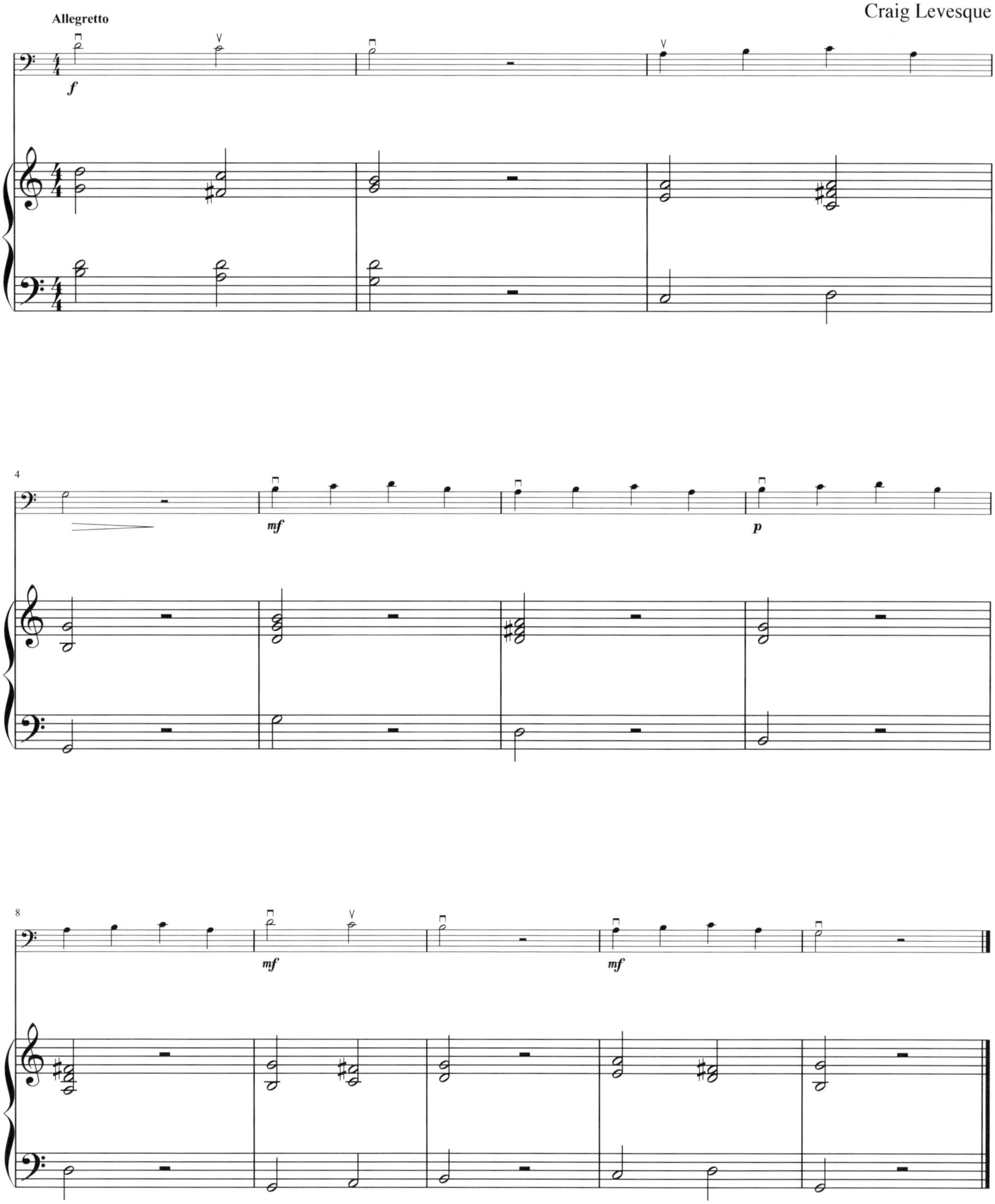

The Hobby Horse

German Folk Song
Craig Levesque

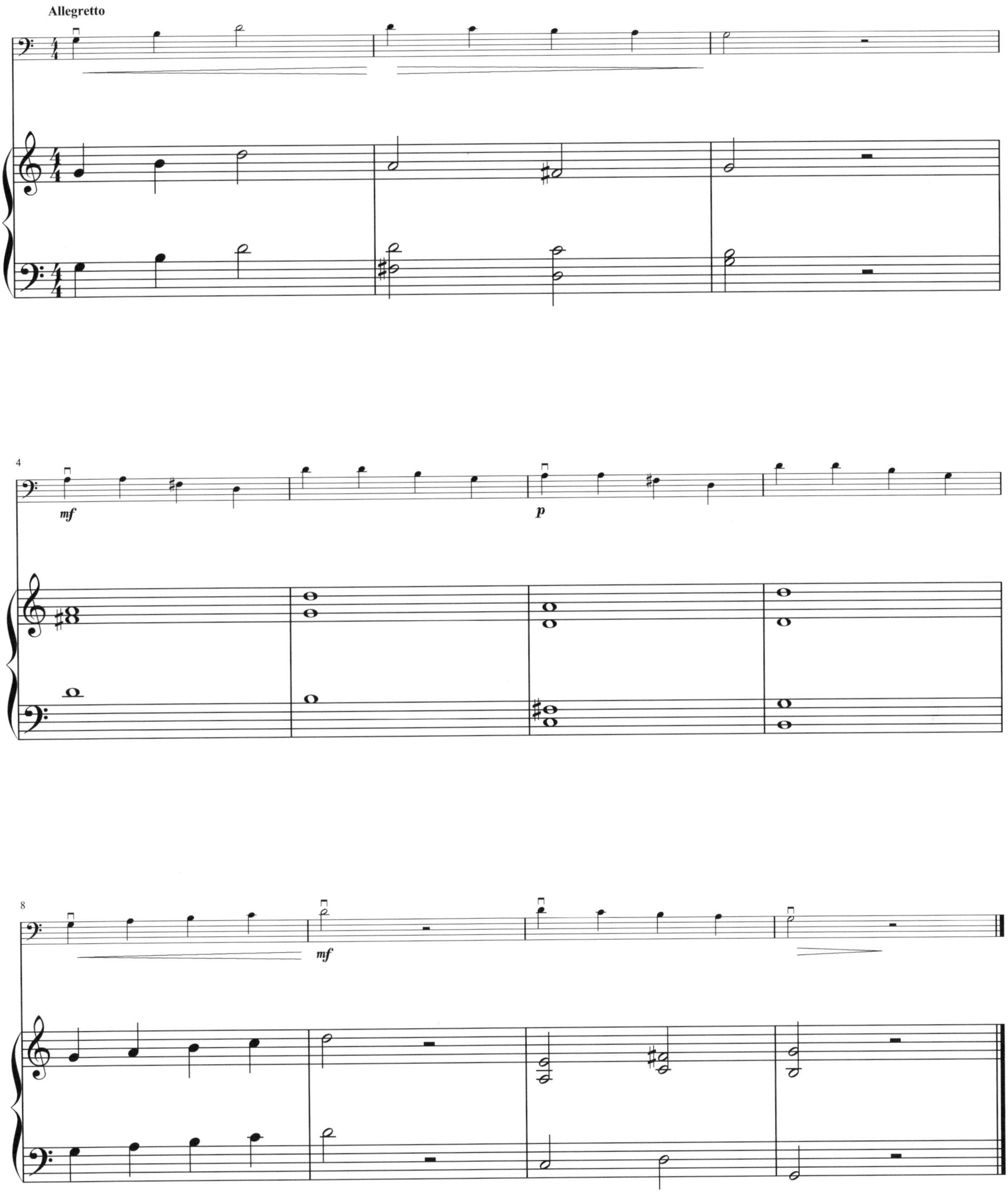

Elephants

Christine Watts
Michi Tashjian

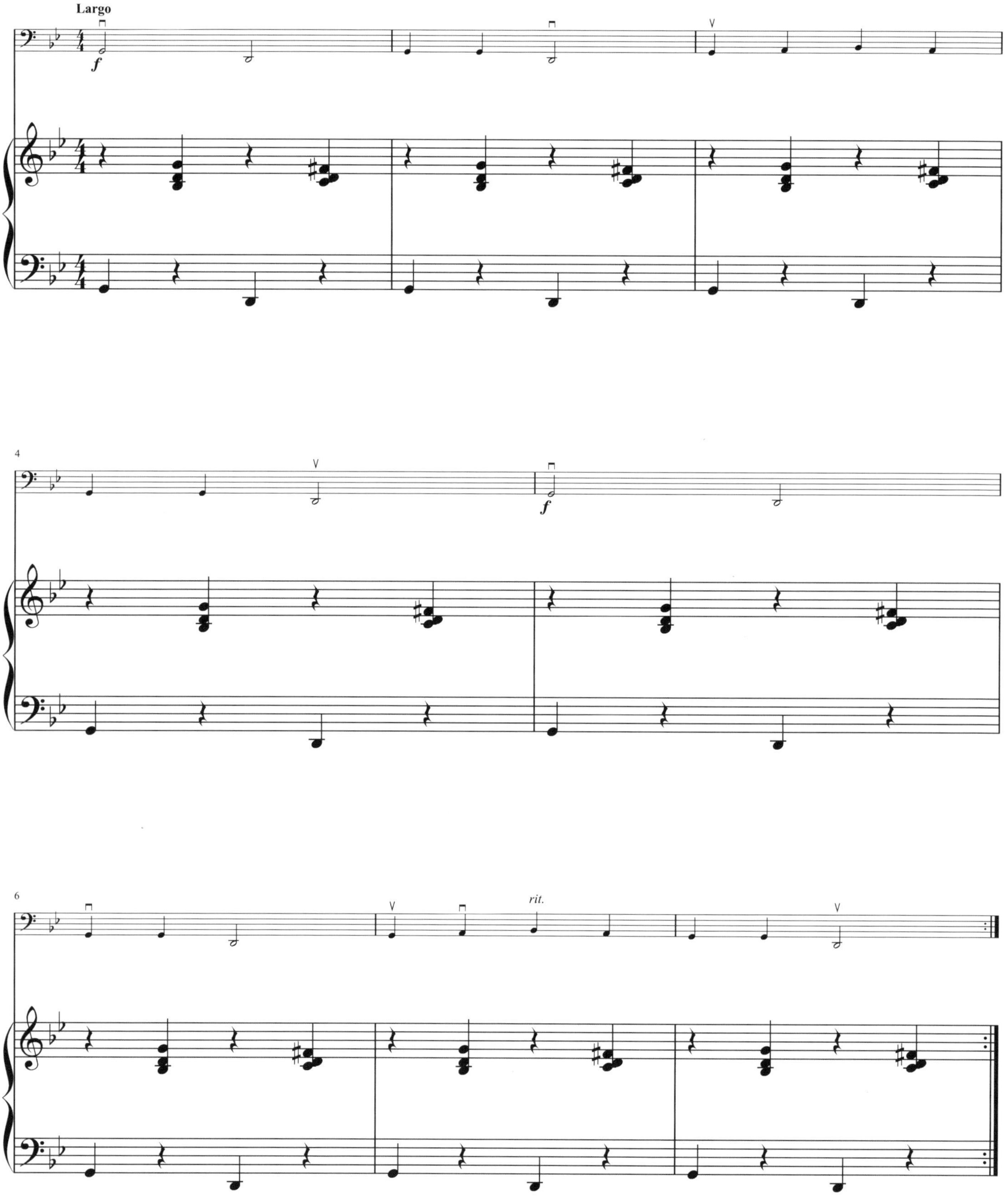

Willie & Tillie

Folk Song
arranged by Sarah Dubois

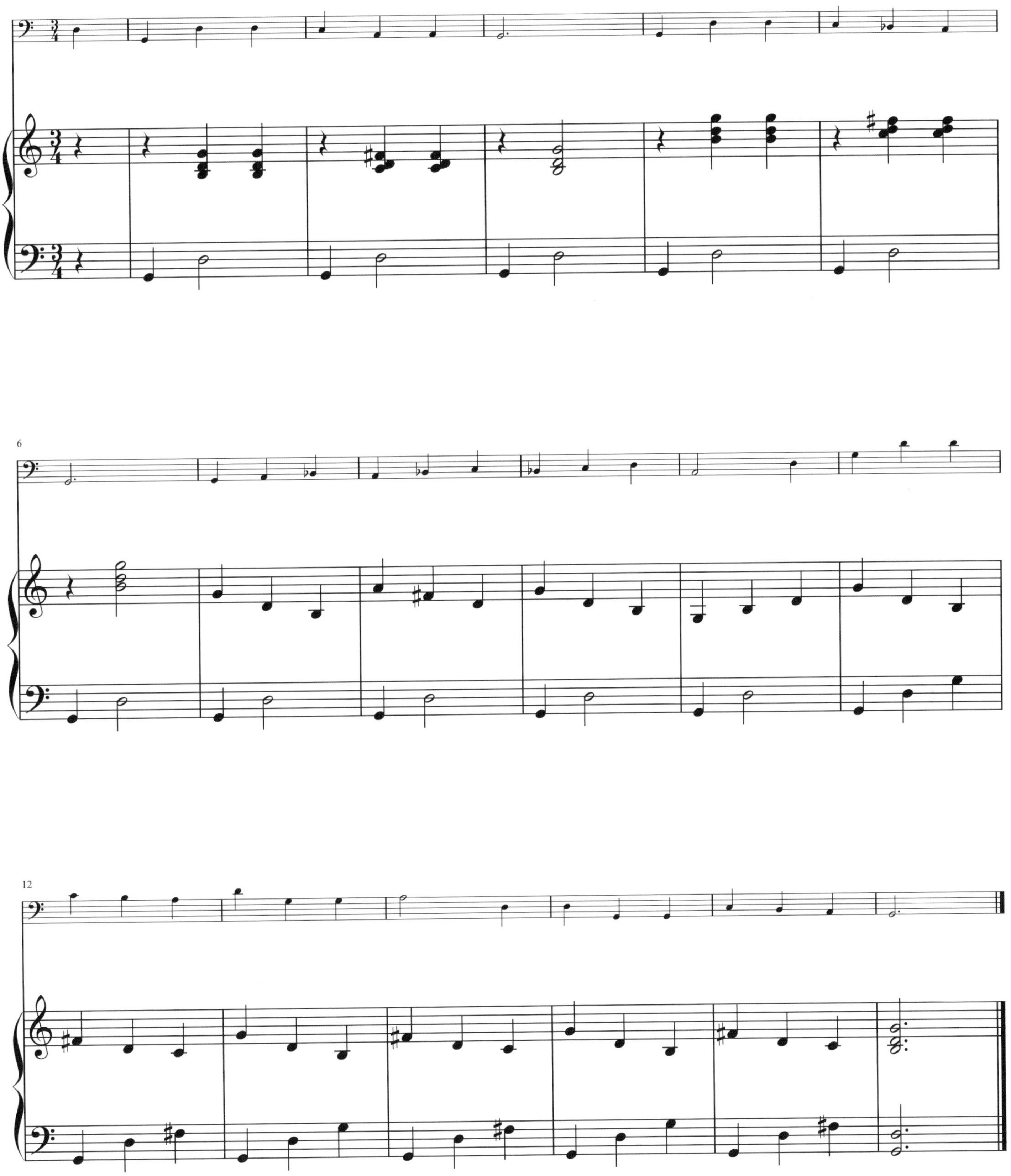

The Cuckoo

English Folk Song
Joseph Kenney

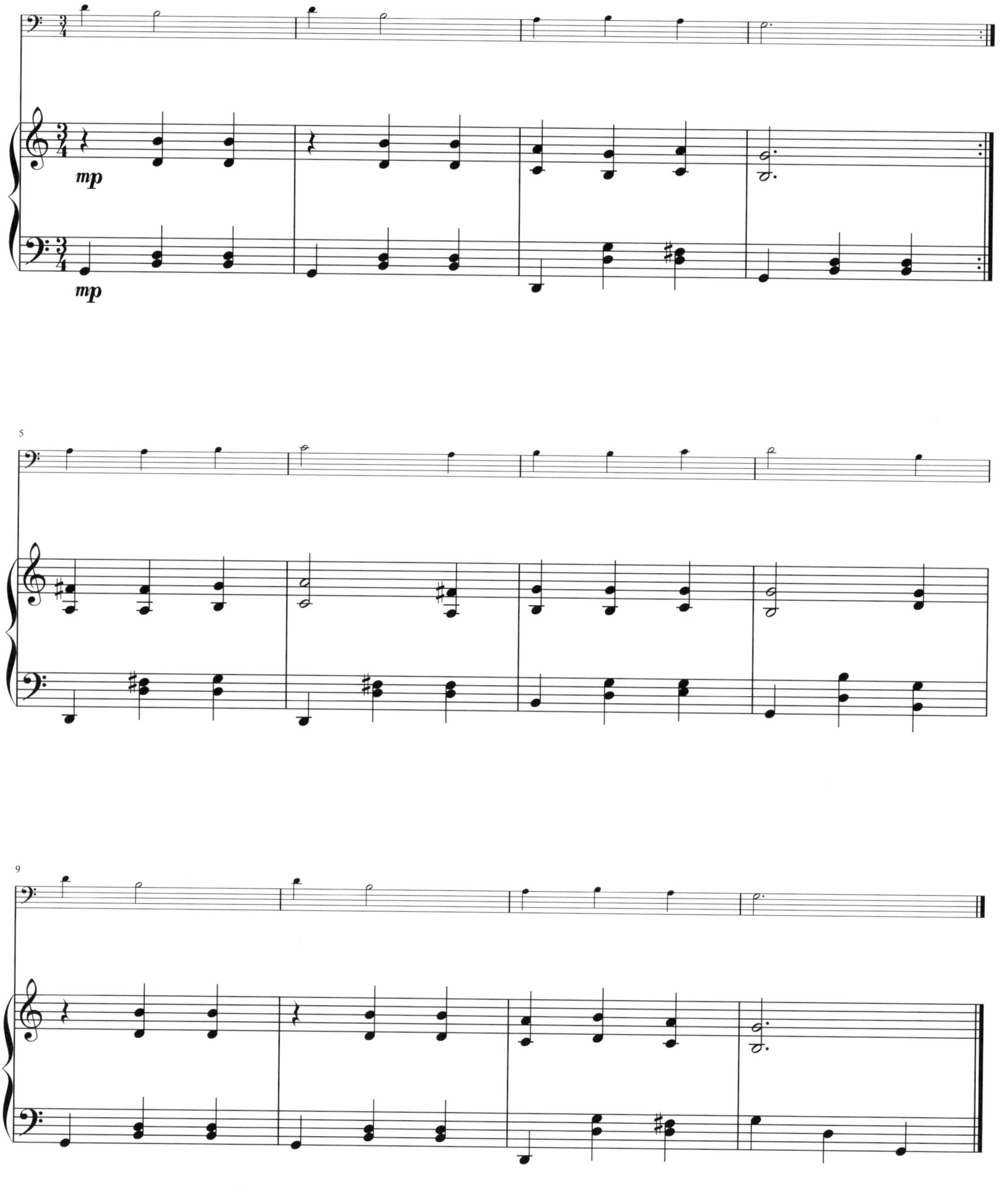

Monkeys Swinging in the Trees

Christine Watts
Joseph Kenney

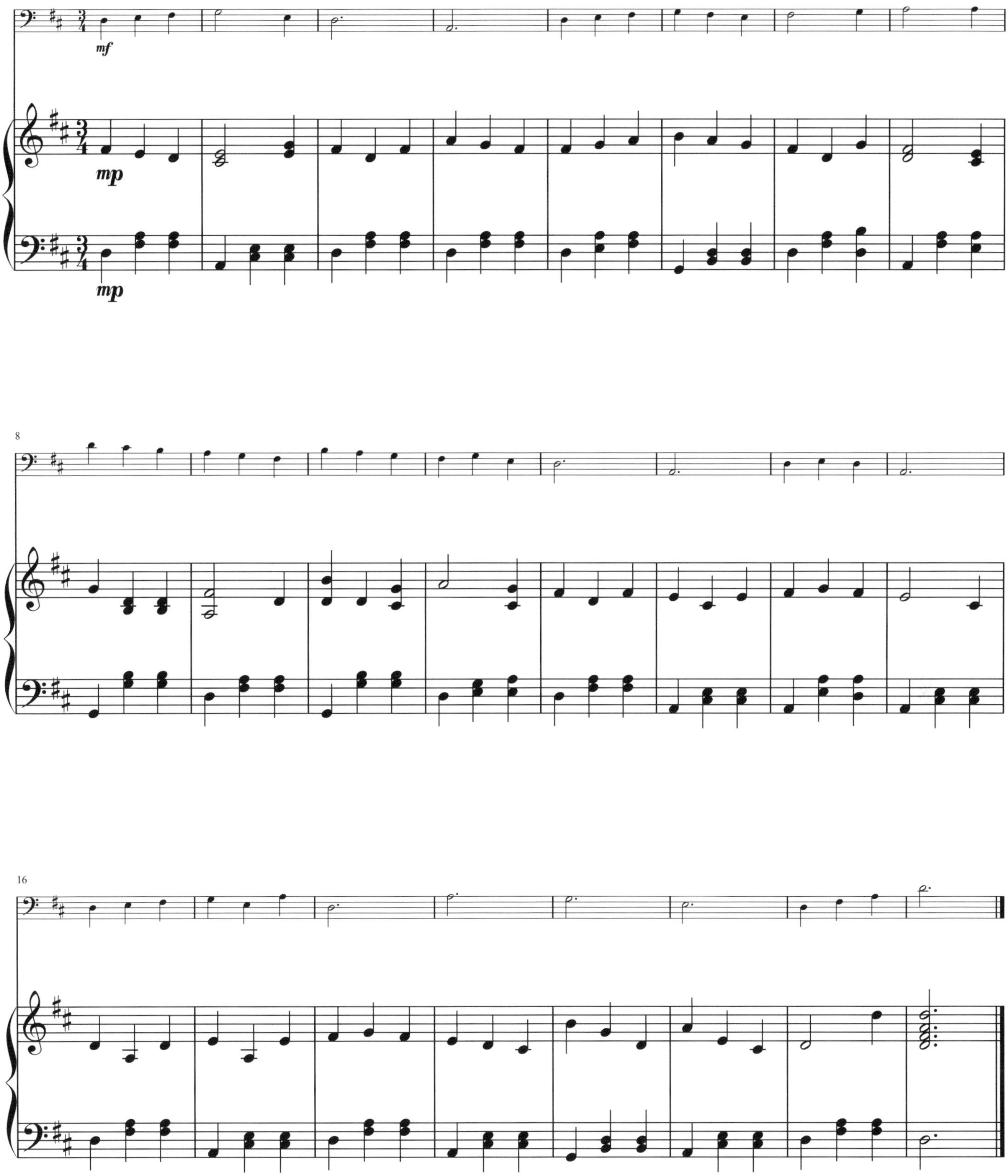

Ladybugs

Christine Watts
Craig Levesque

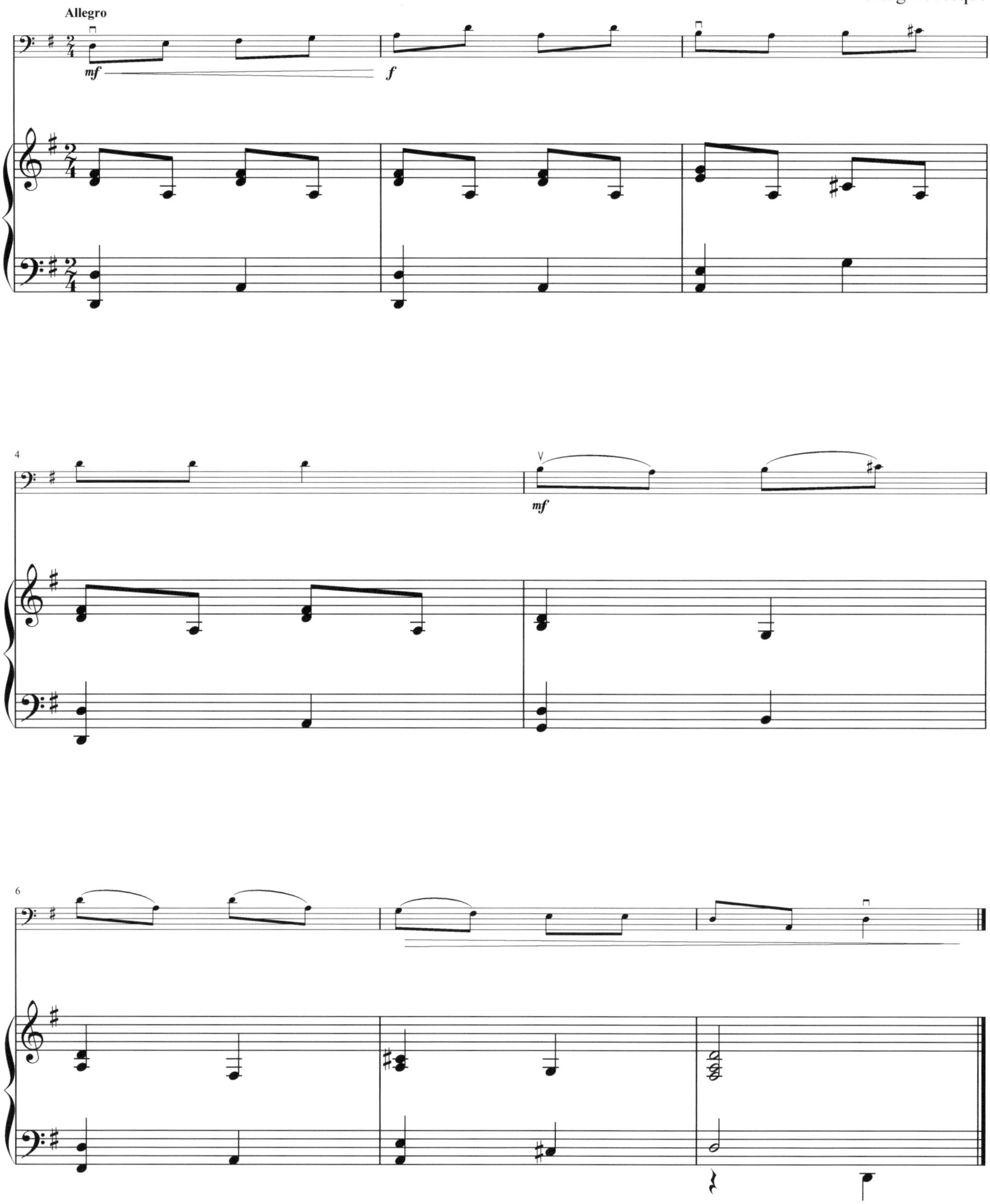

Ladybug Fly Away

American Folk Song
Craig Levesque

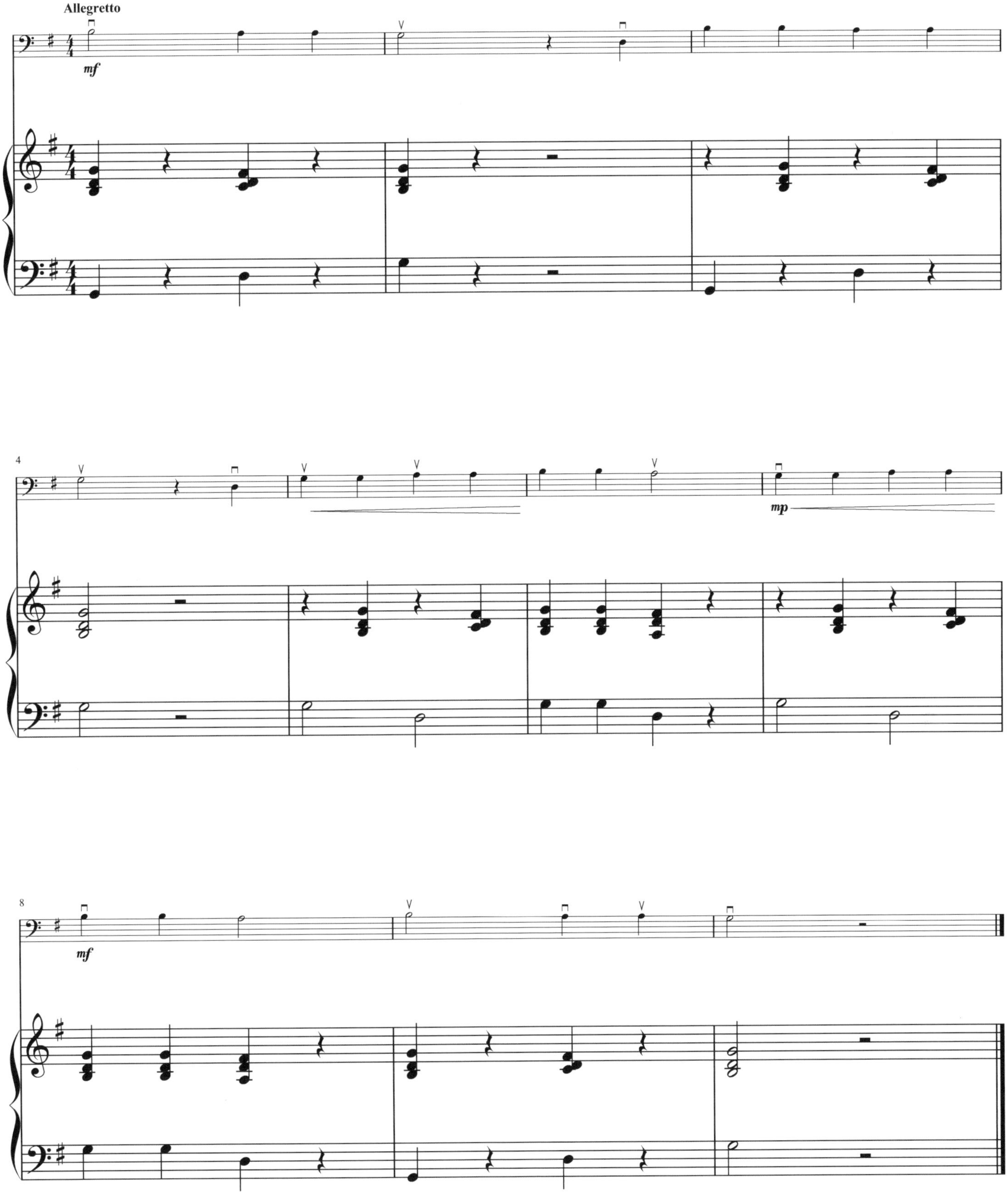

The Contented Cow

Christine Watts
Joseph Kenney

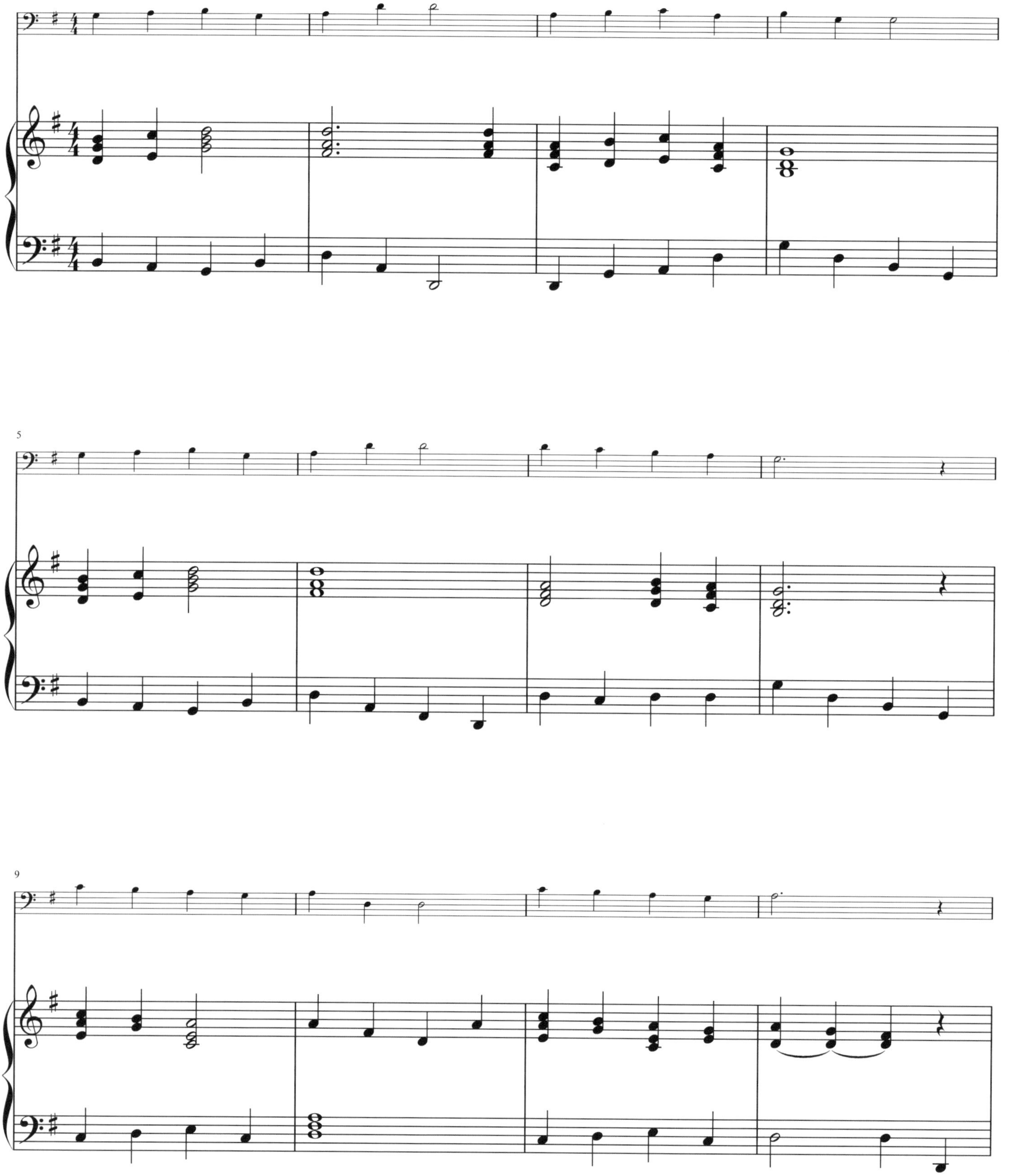

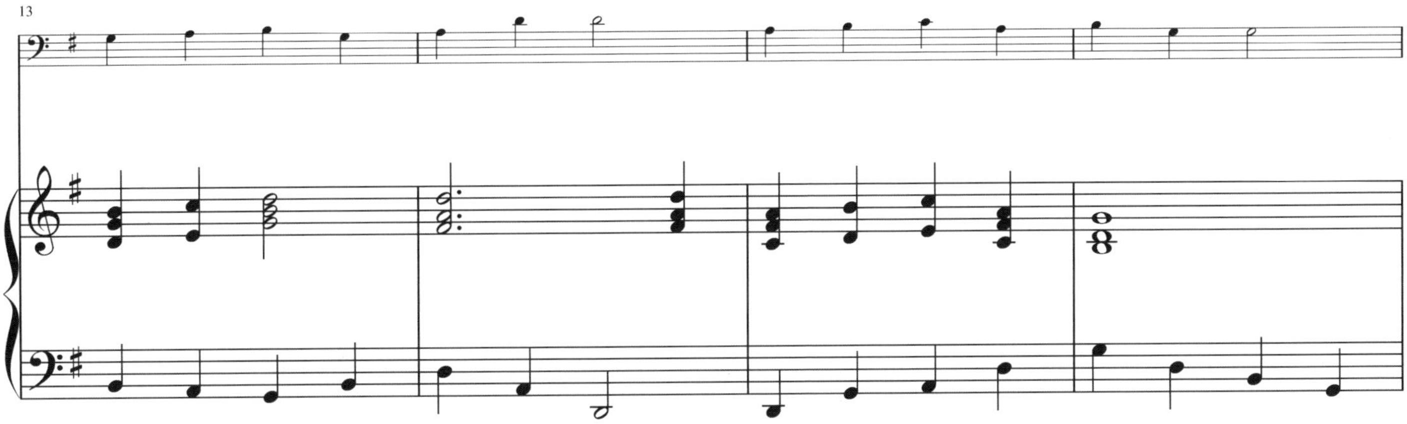
13

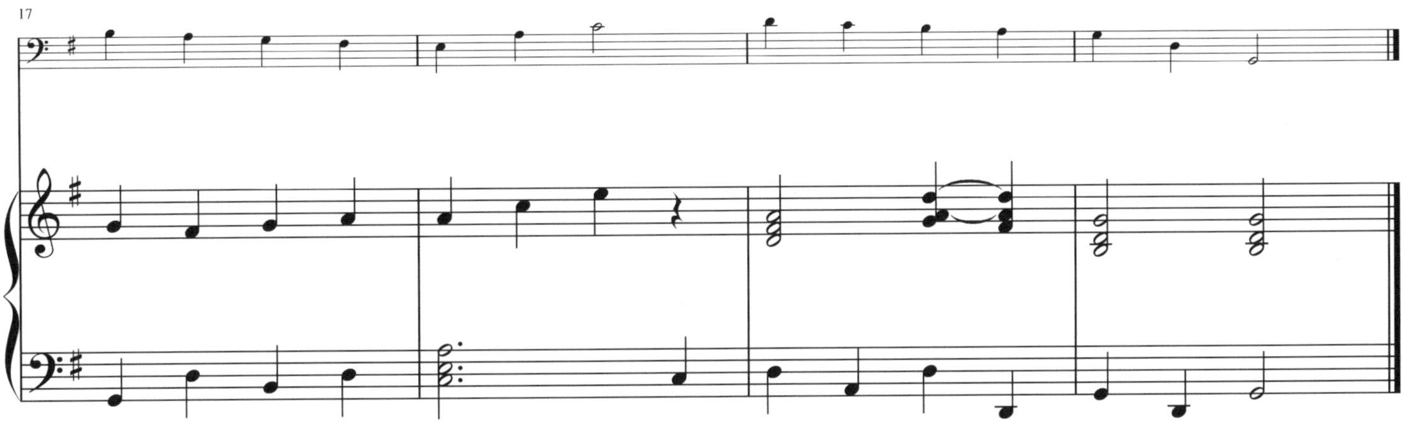
17

This page has been left blank
to avoid awkward page turns.

Country Dance

Beethoven
Joseph Kenney

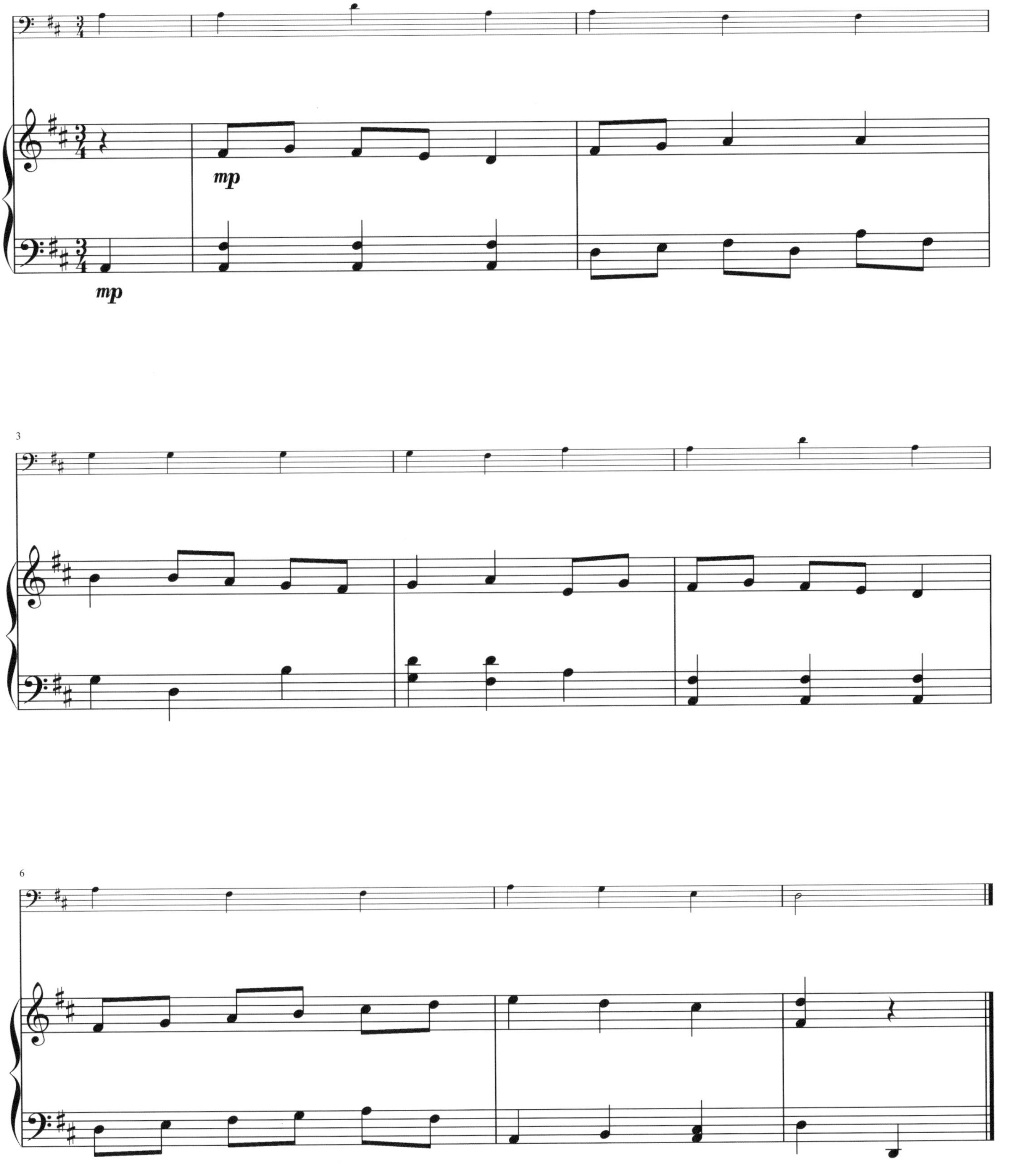

The Clever Fox

Polish Folk Song
Joseph Kenney

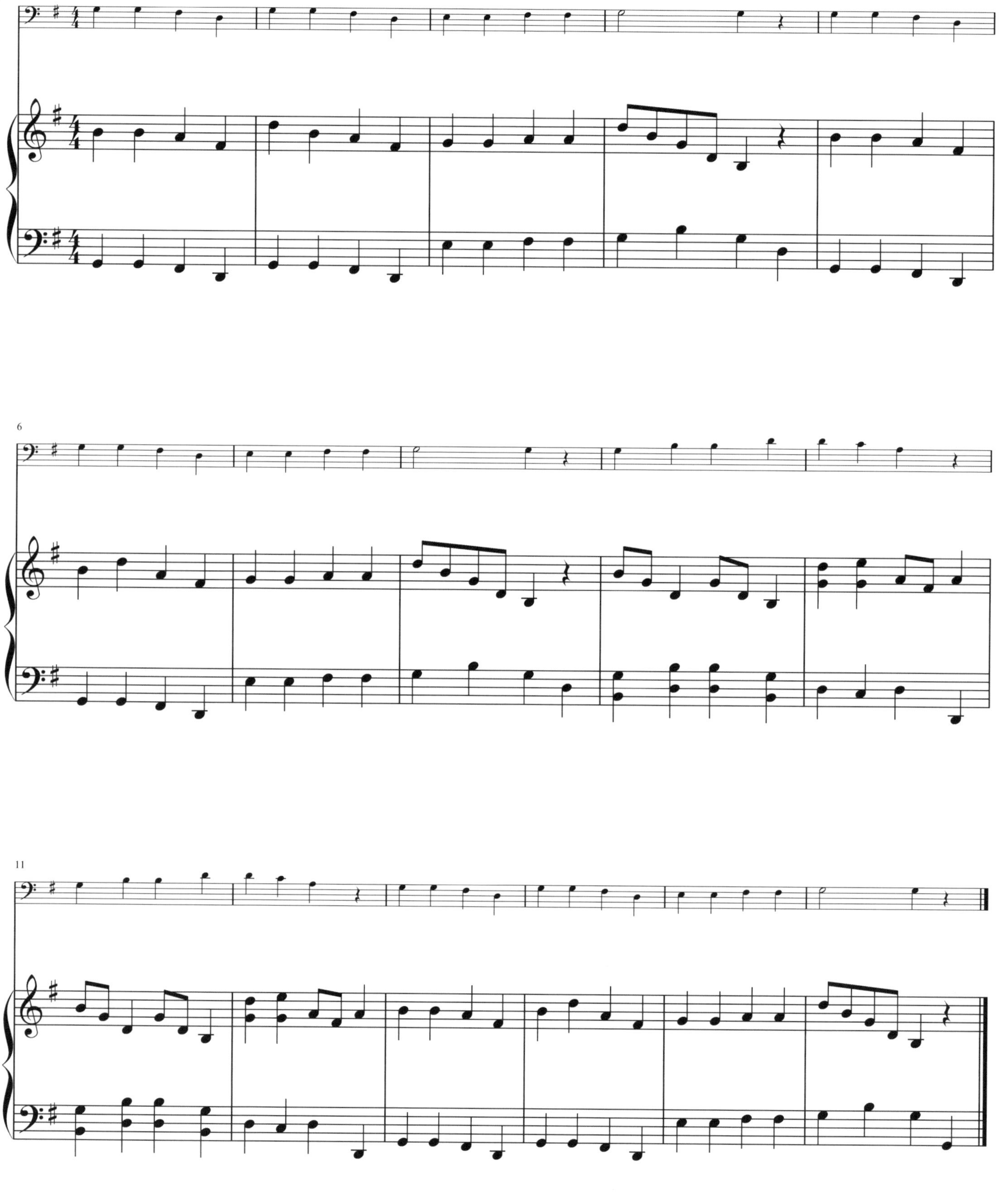

The Zebra's Dance

Christine Watts
Michi Tashjian

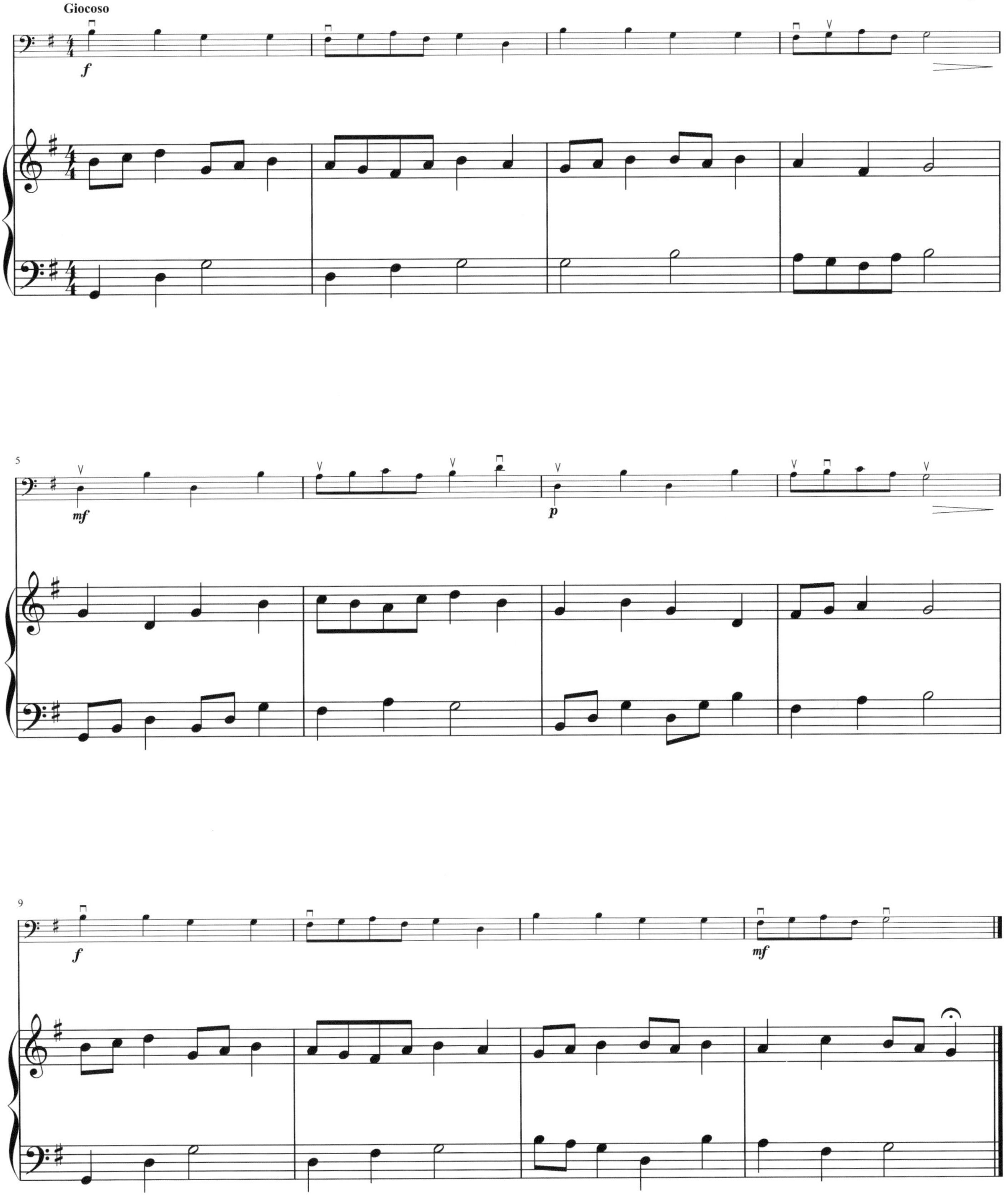

Sister Come Dance With Me

American Folk Song
Craig Levesque

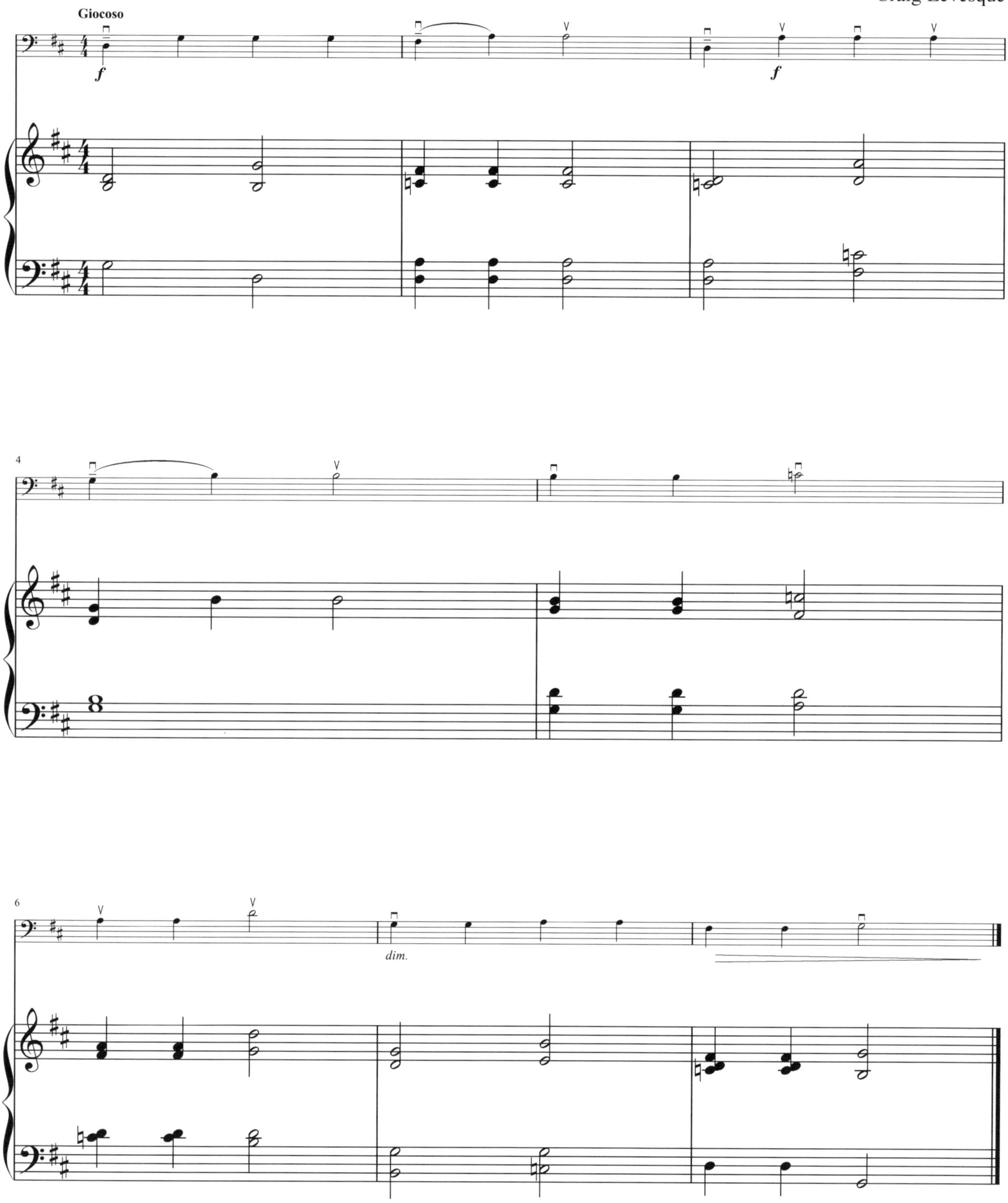

This page has been left blank
to avoid awkward page turns.

The Drum

William Duncombe
Joseph Kenney

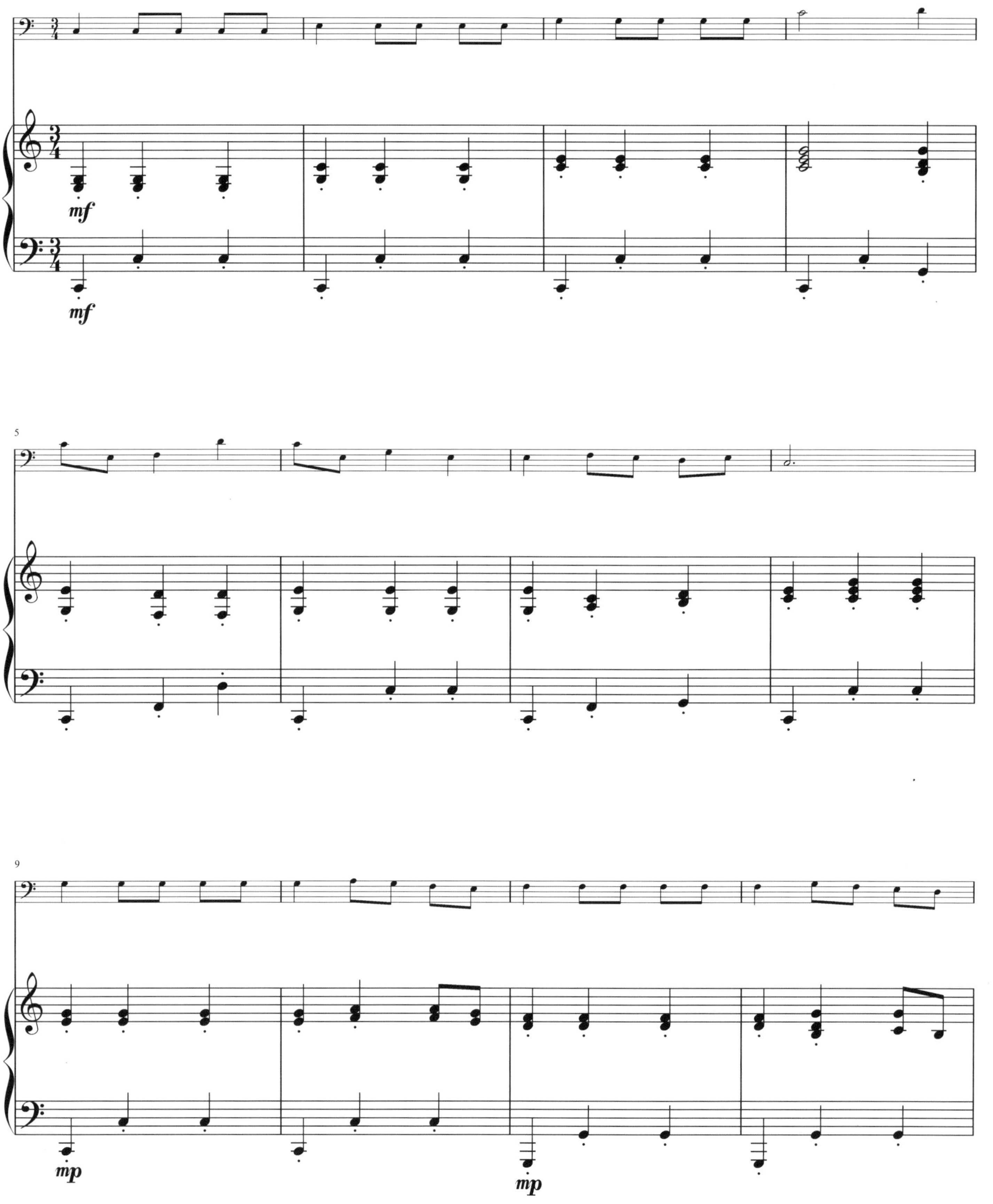

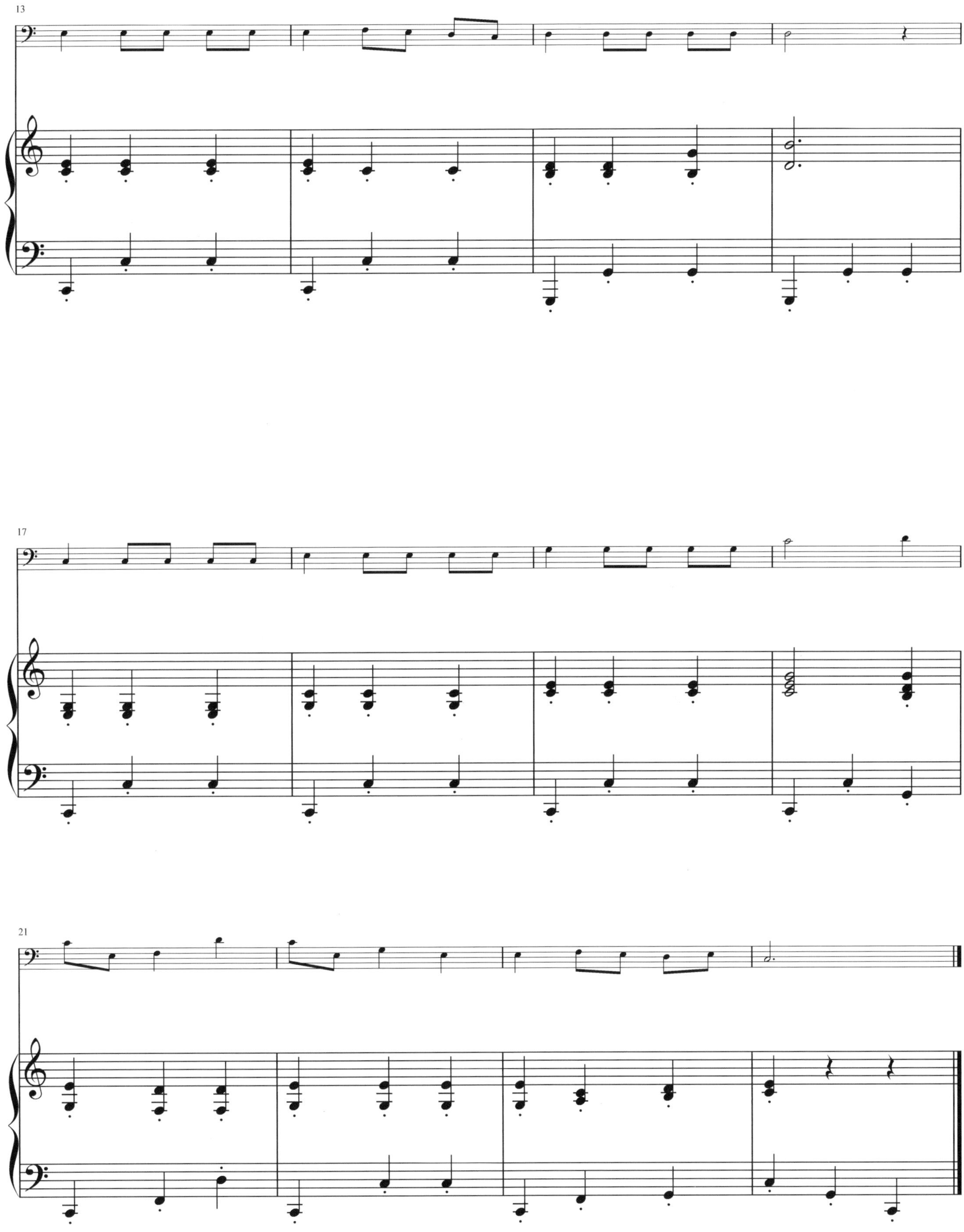
13
17
21

Laughing Song

("Die Fledermaus," Opera act II)

Johann Strauss II
Craig Levesque

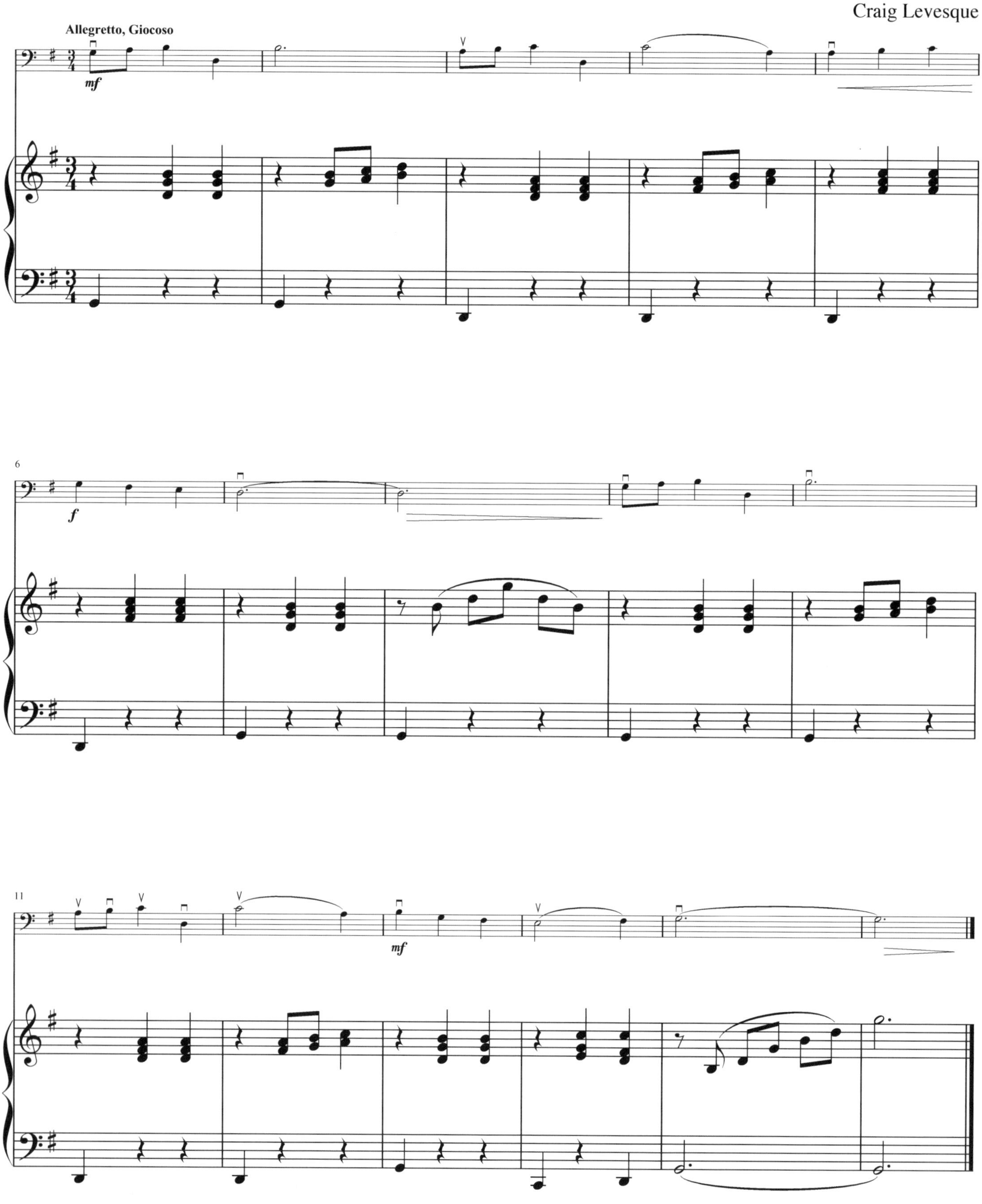

The Magic Ring

Old Lithuanian Song
Michi Tashjian

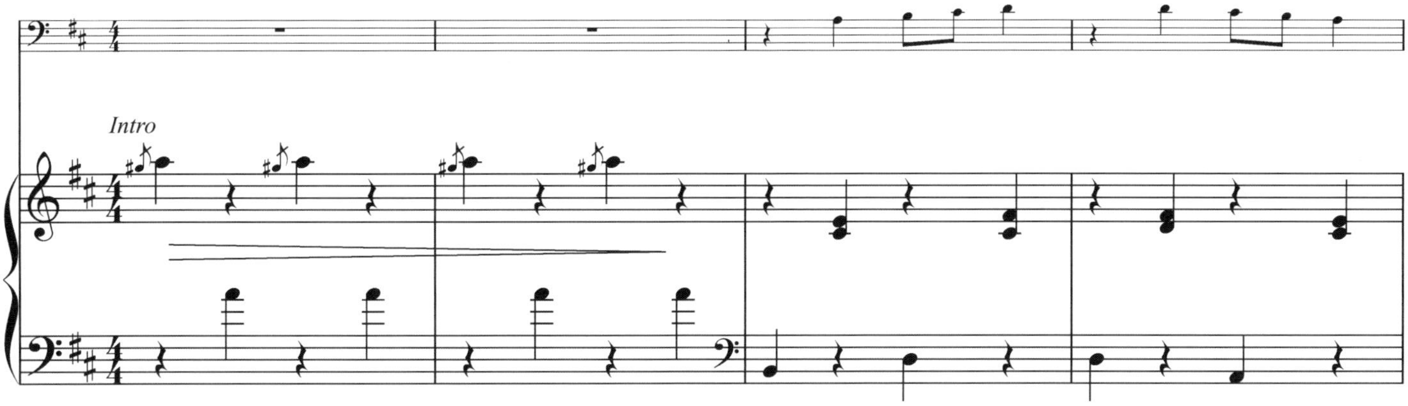

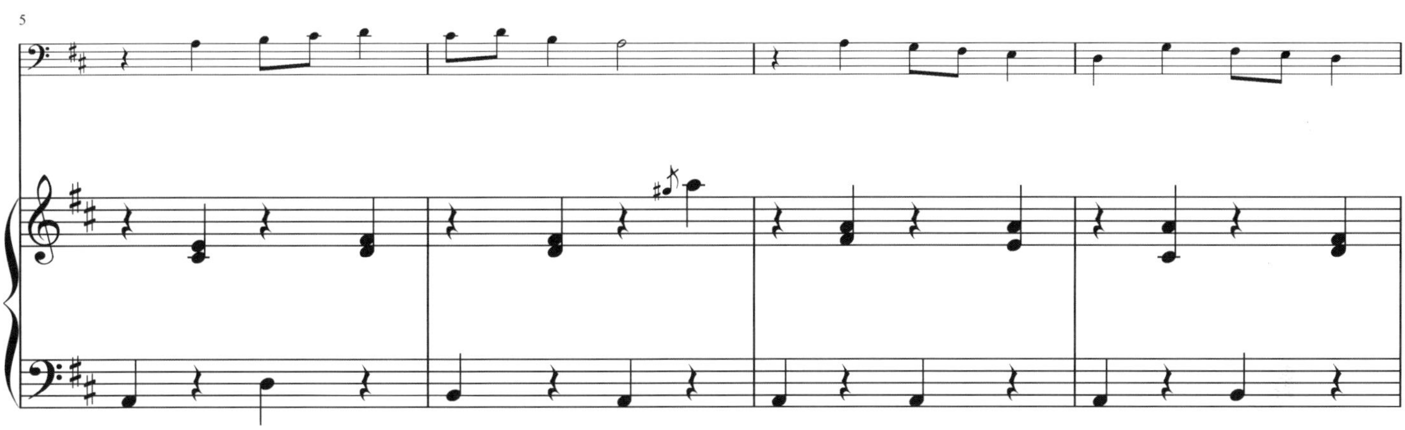

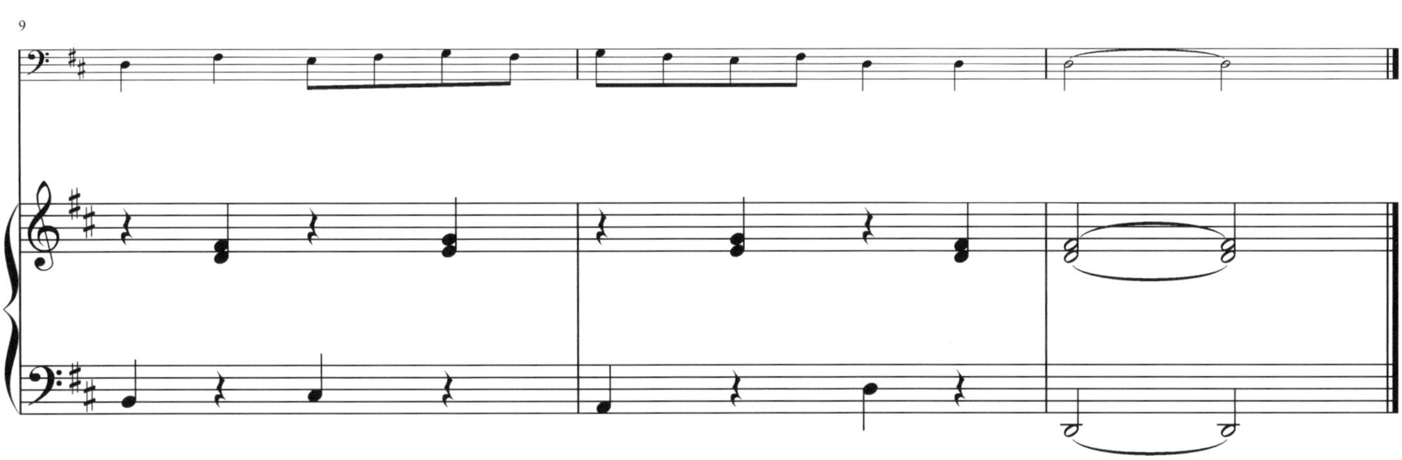

Minuet in G

Joseph Haydn
Craig Levesque

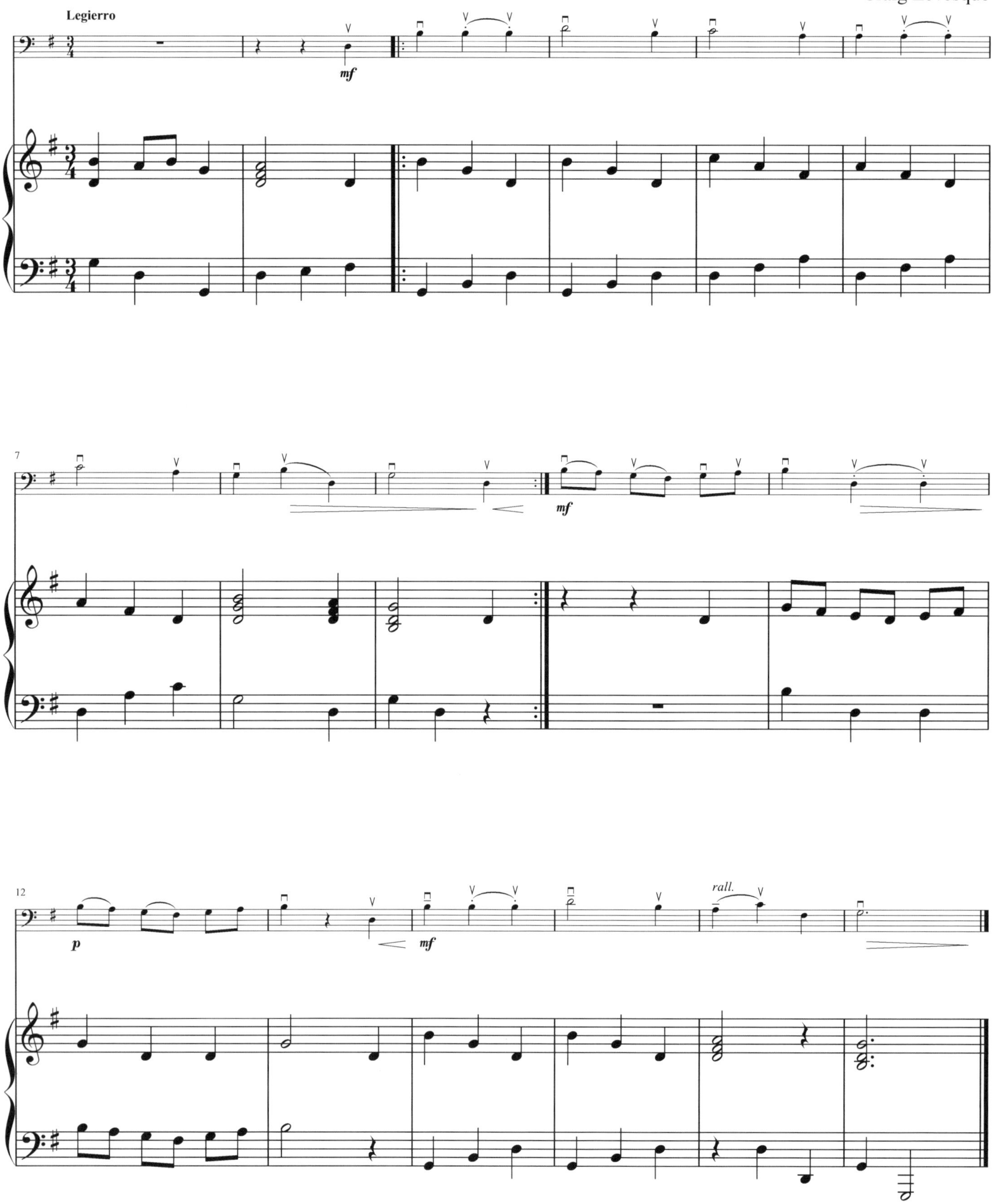

The Dancing Dog

Christine Watts
Craig Levesque

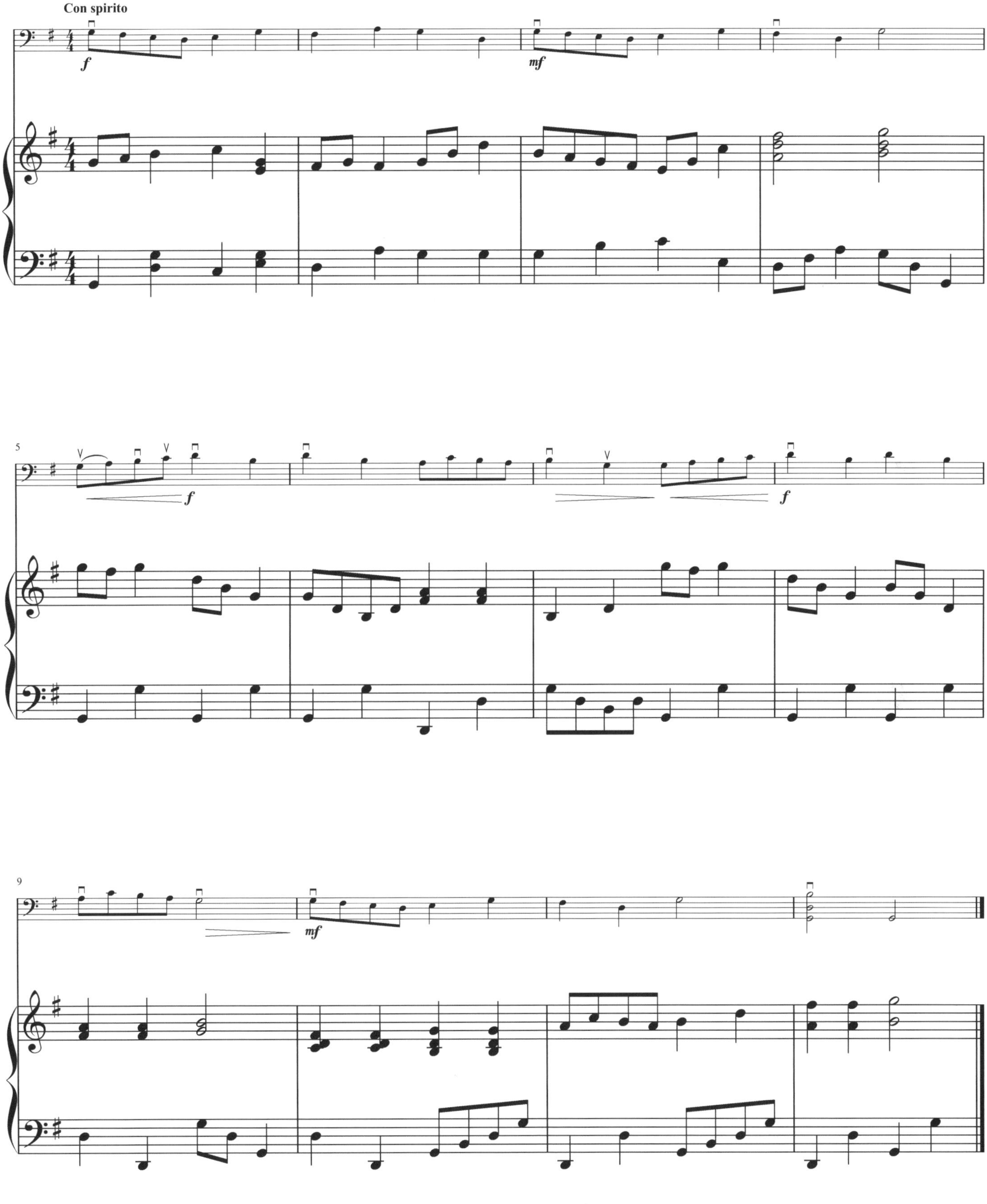

Between the Ox and the Donkey

American Folk Song
Craig Levesque

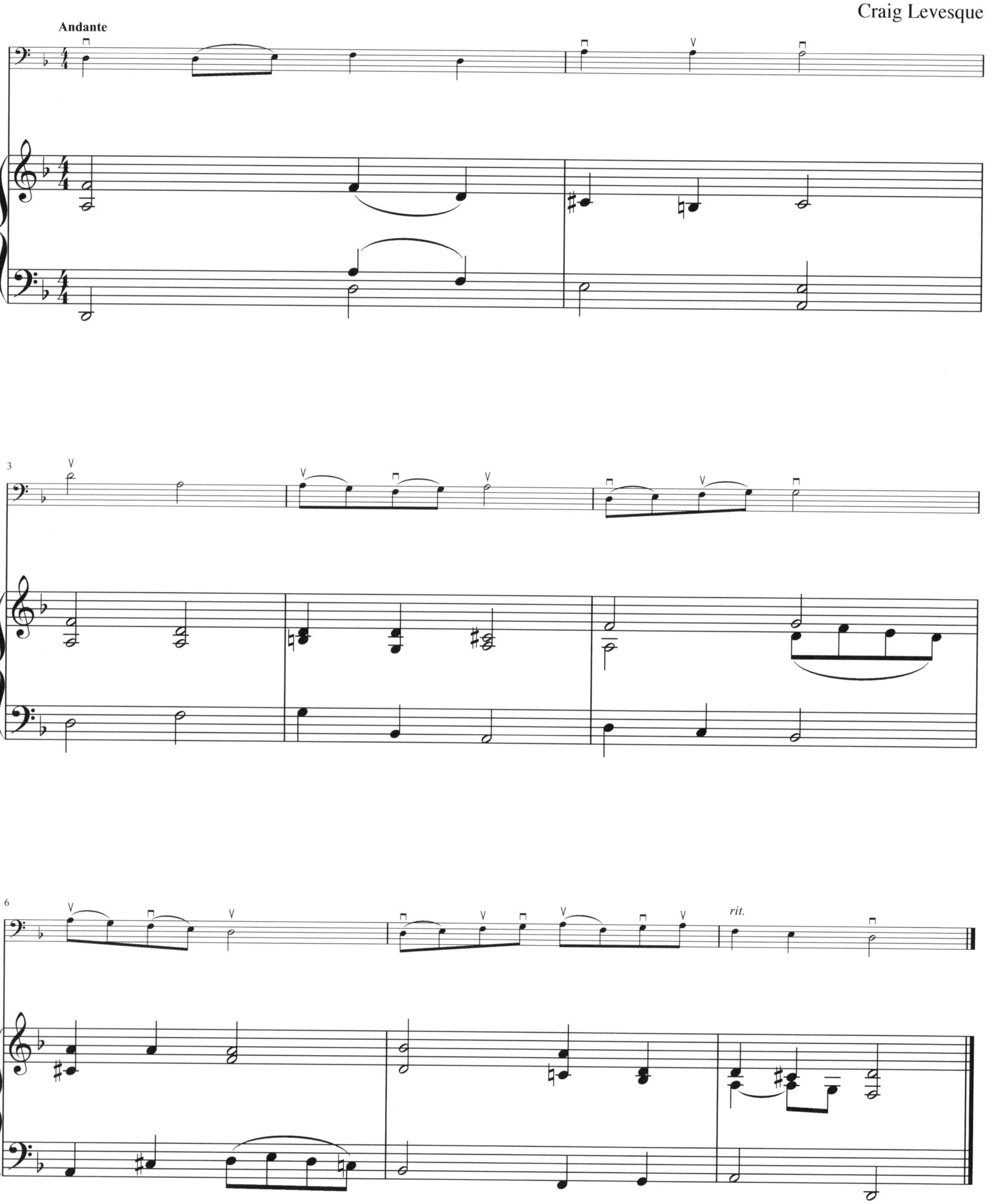

Country Fair Day

Christine Watts
Michi Tashjian

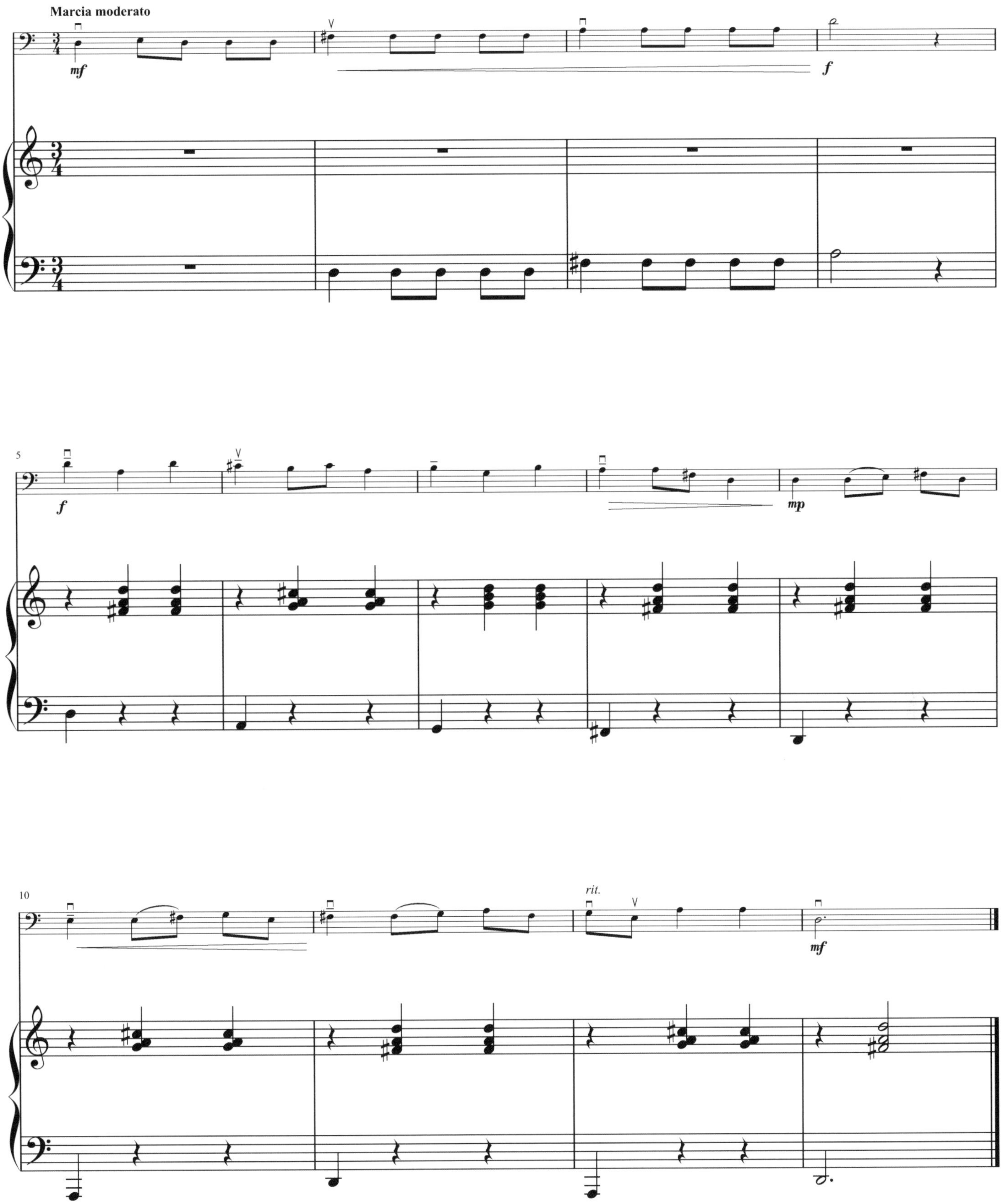

This page has been left blank
to avoid awkward page turns.

The Little Fiddle

American Folk Song
Craig Levesque

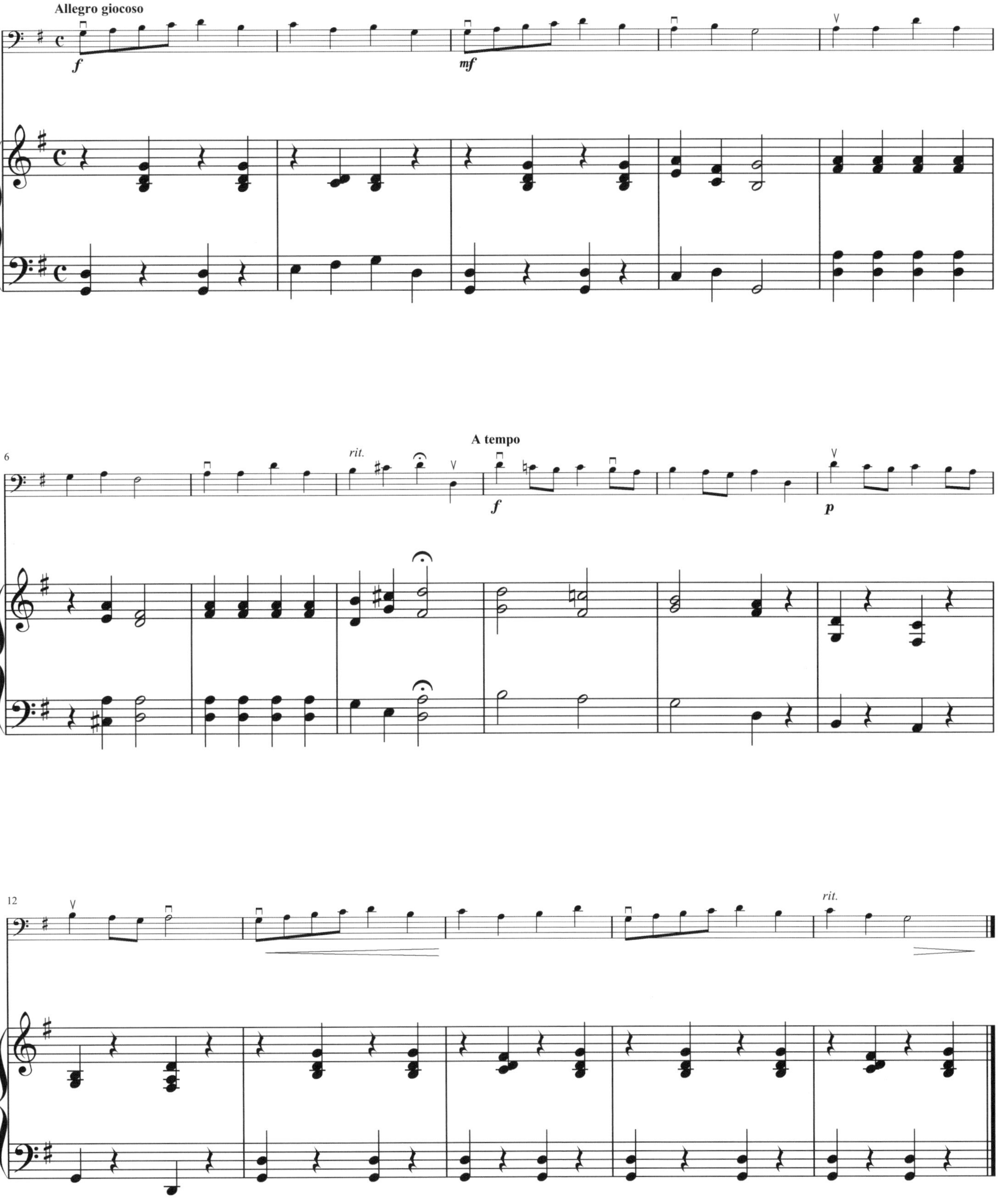

Evening Song

Welsh Air
Craig Levesque

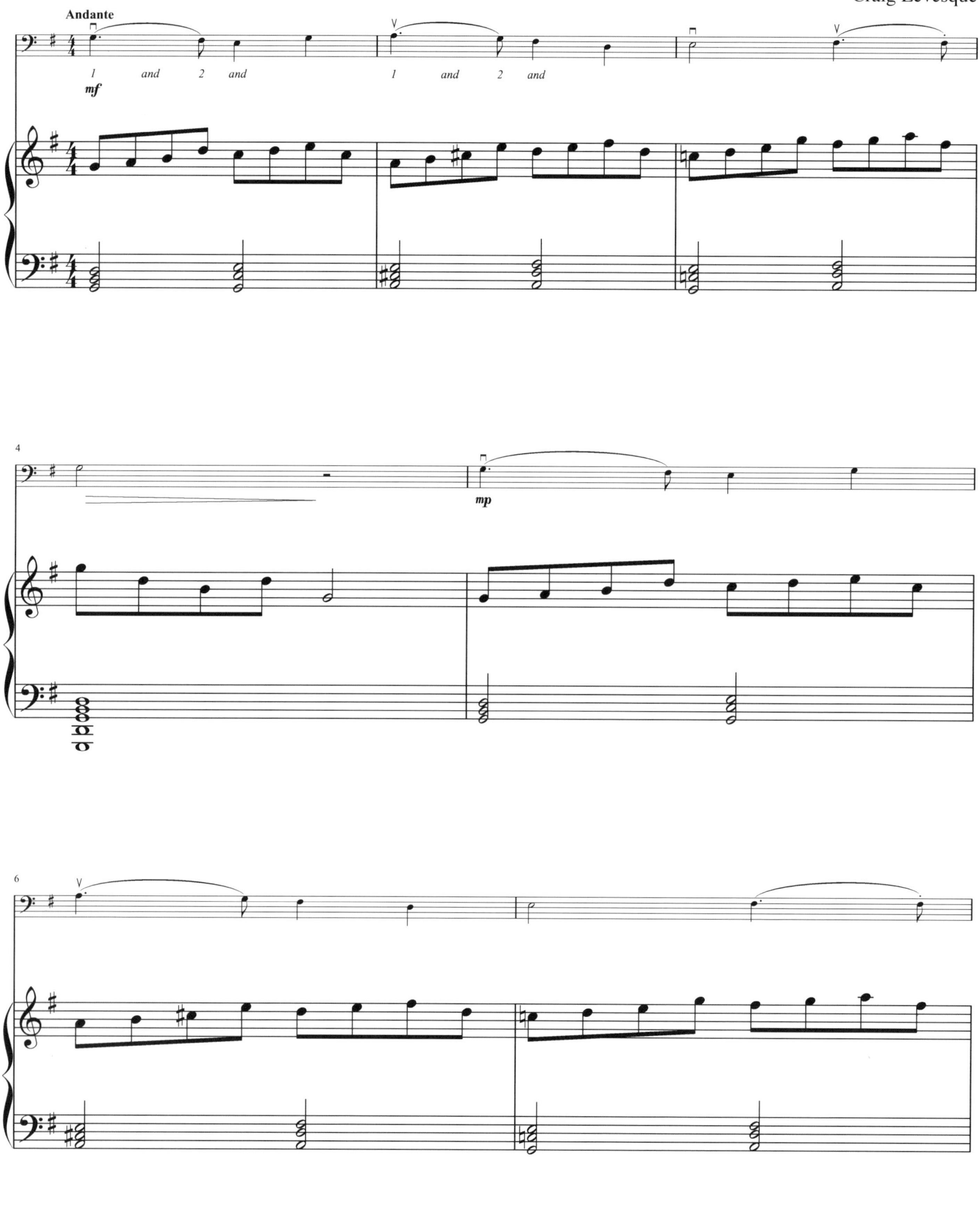

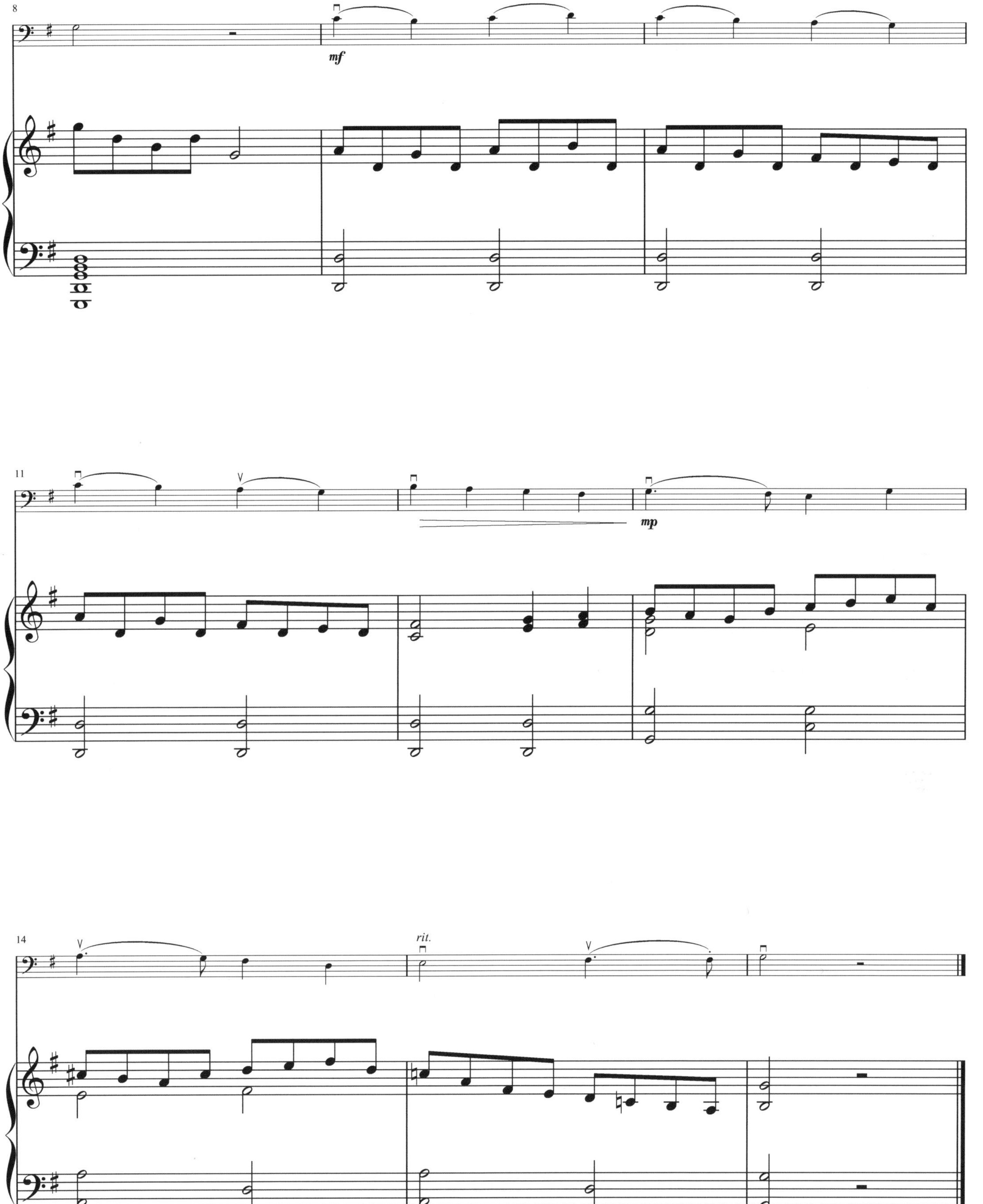
8
mf
11
mp
14
rit.

Eine Klein Nachtmusik

W. A. Mozart
Michi Tashjian

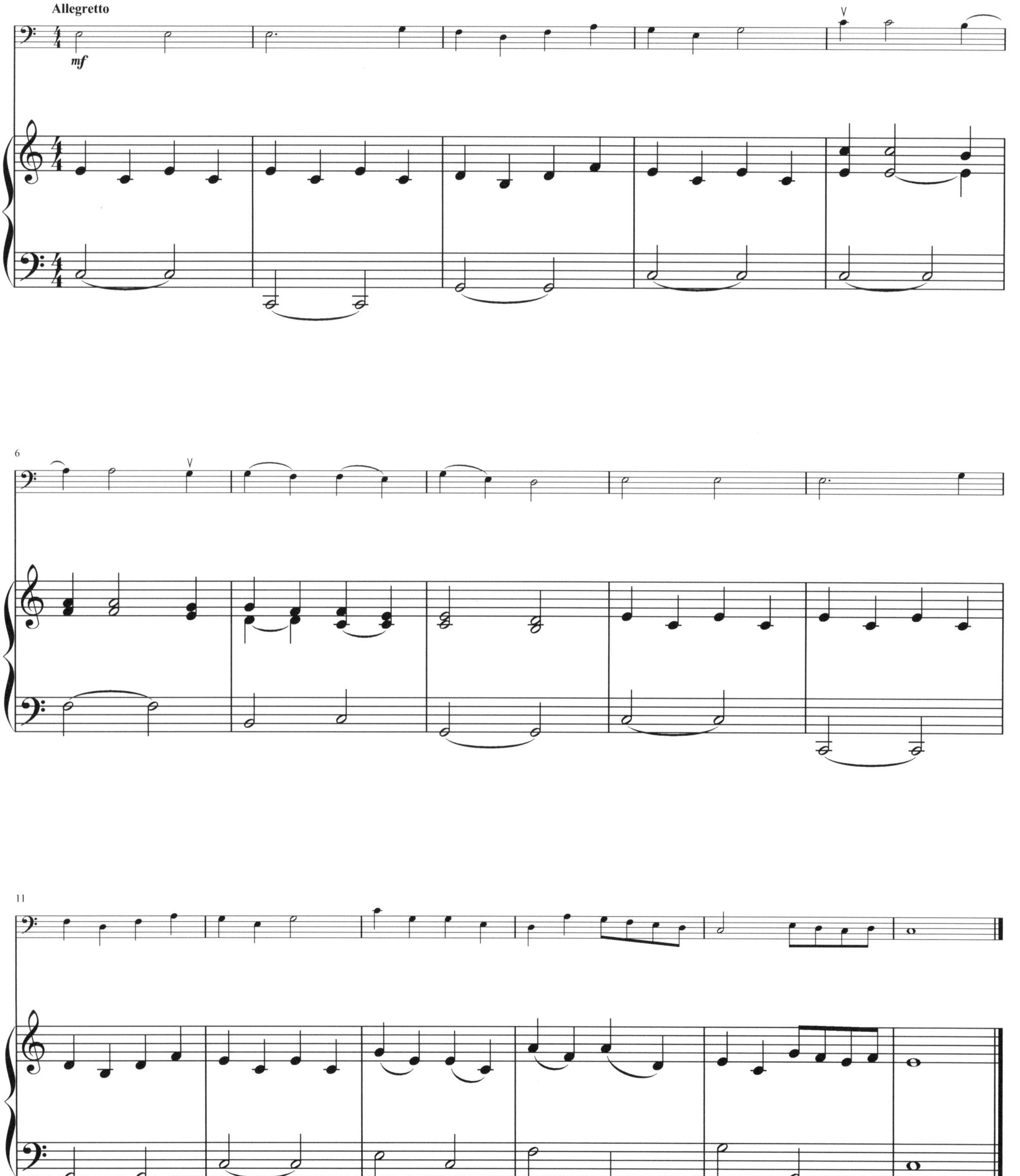

Barnyard Secrets

Christine Watts
Michi Tashjian

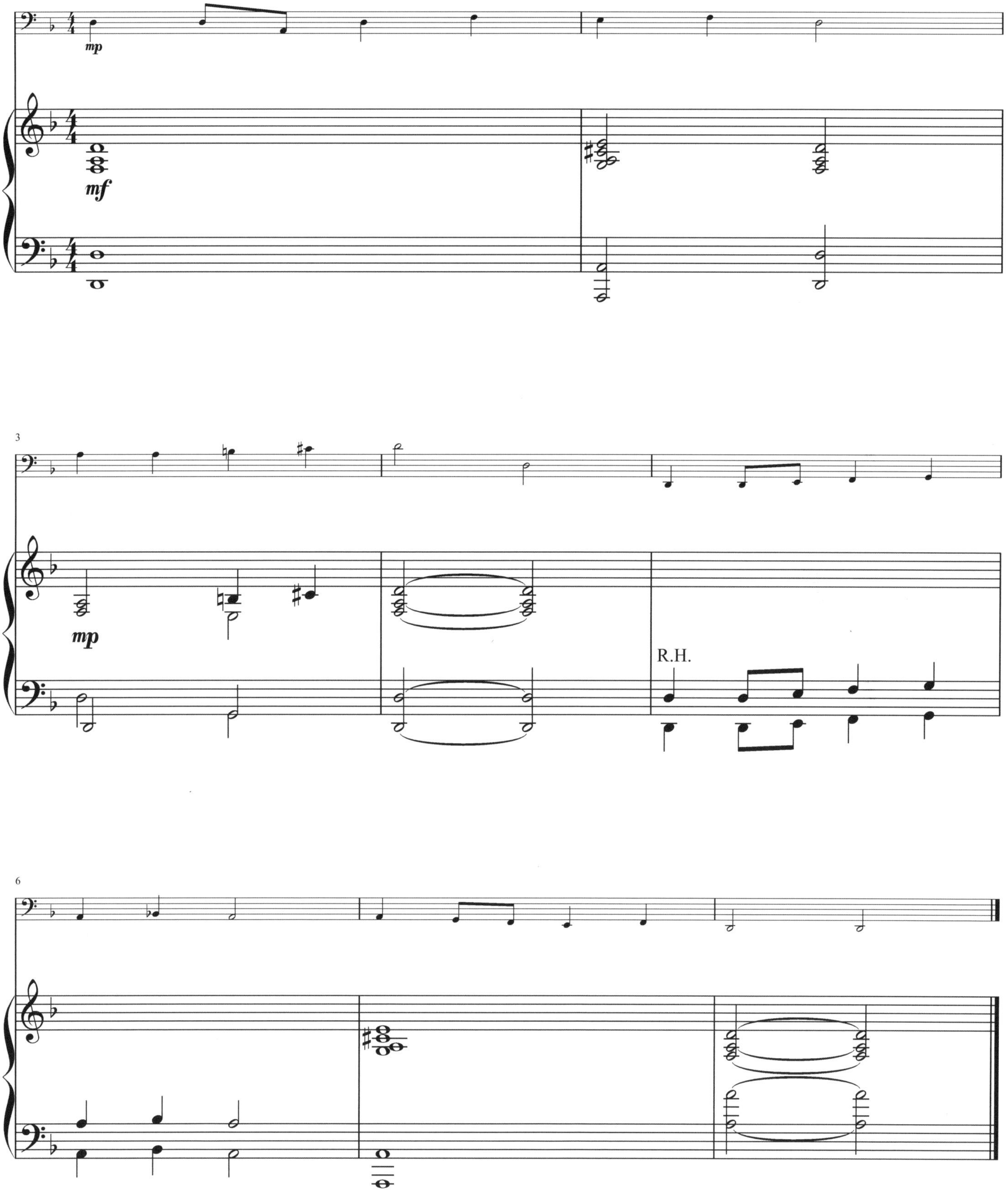

German Dance

W. A. Mozart
Craig Levesque

Moderato, Energico

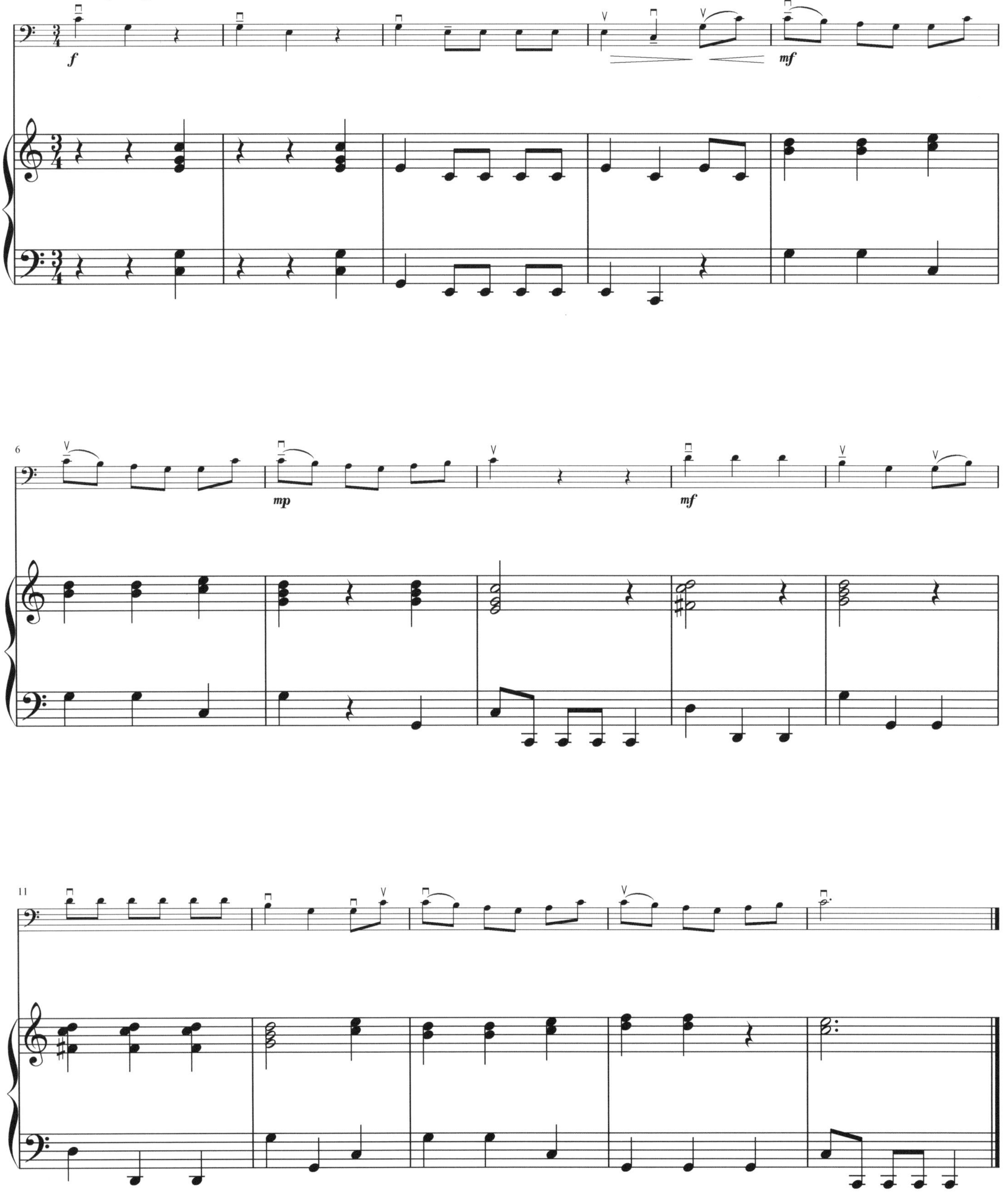

The Cool, Clear Pond

Folk Song
Craig Levesque

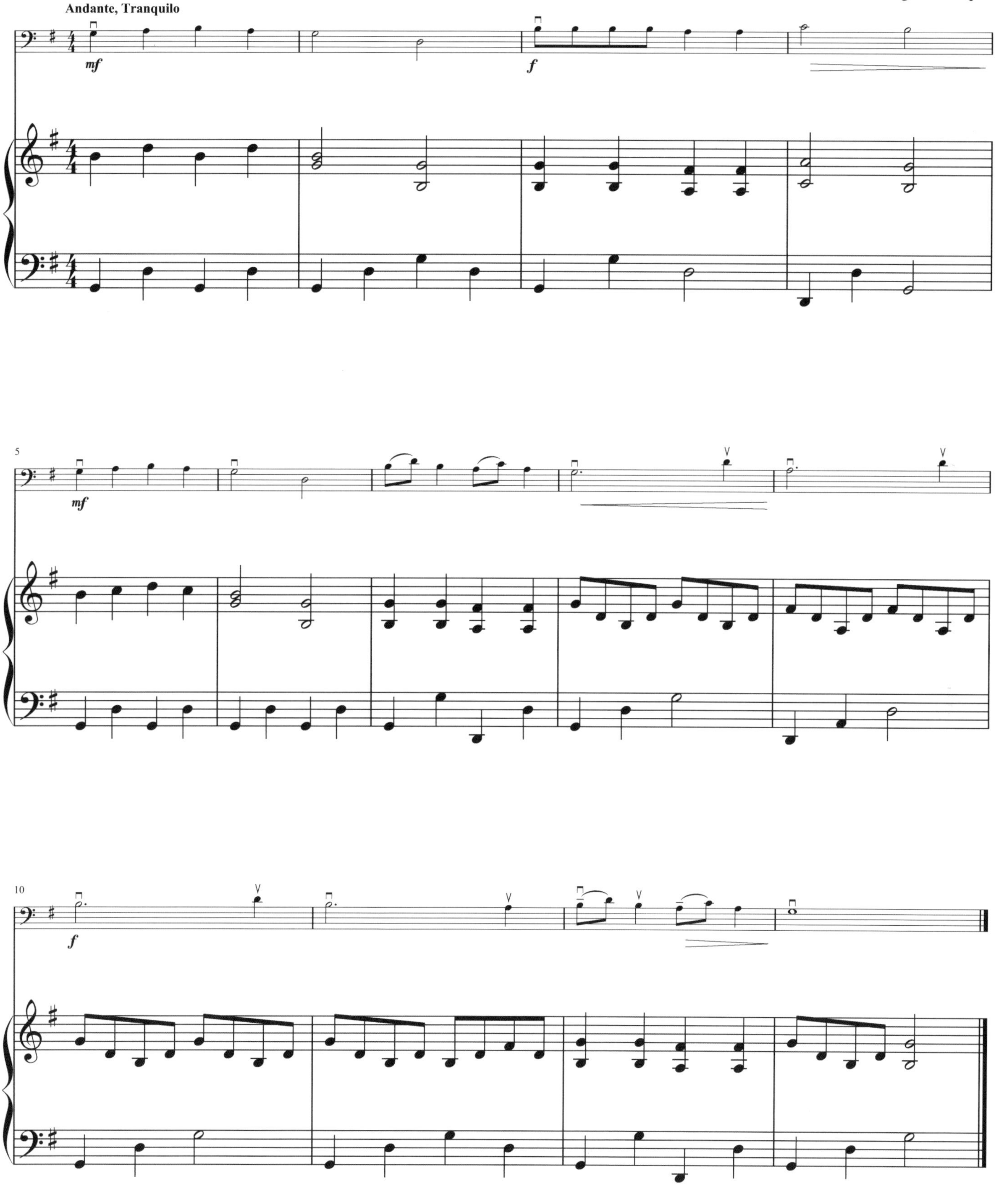

Beautiful Dreamer

Stephen Foster
Michi Tashjian

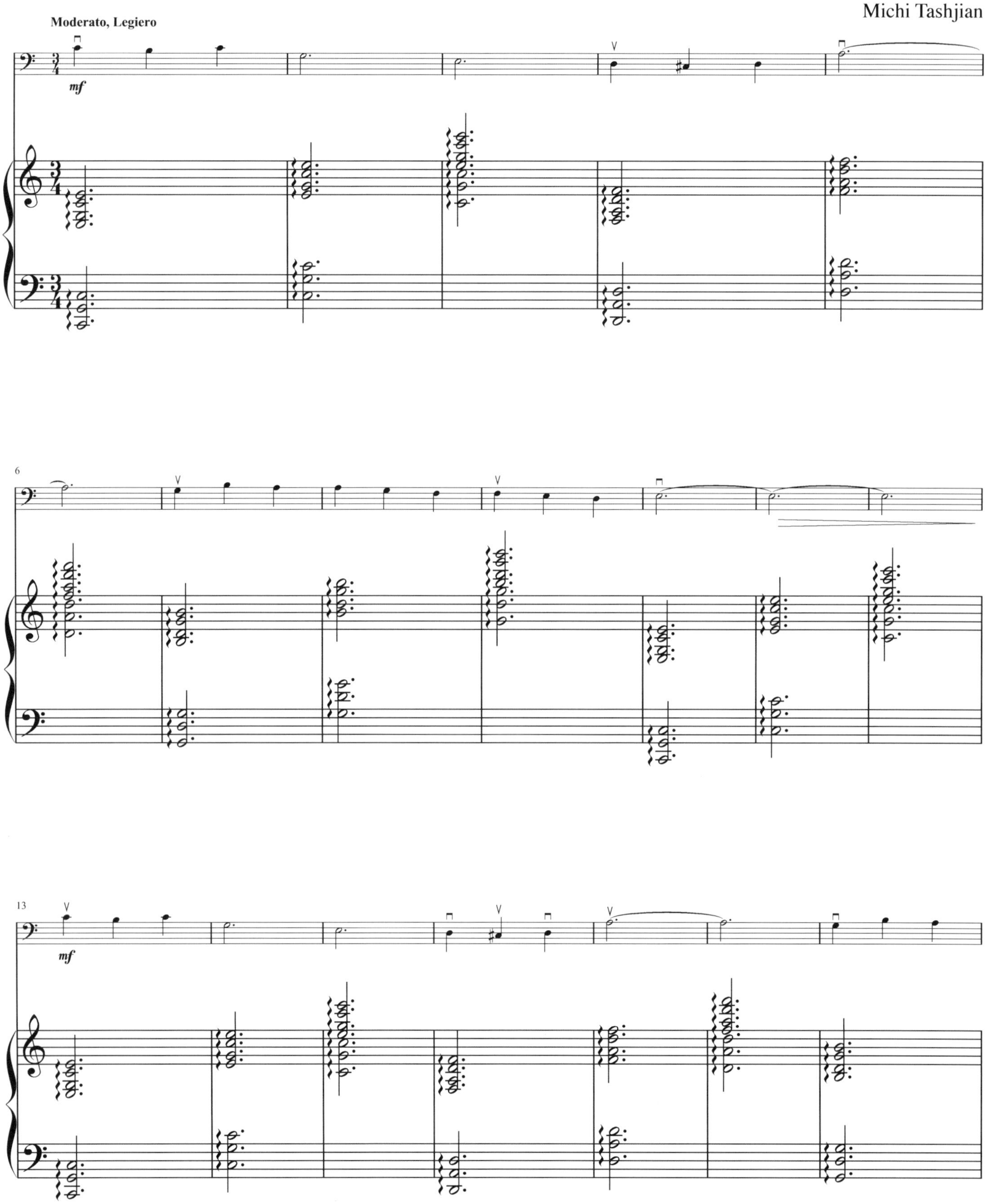

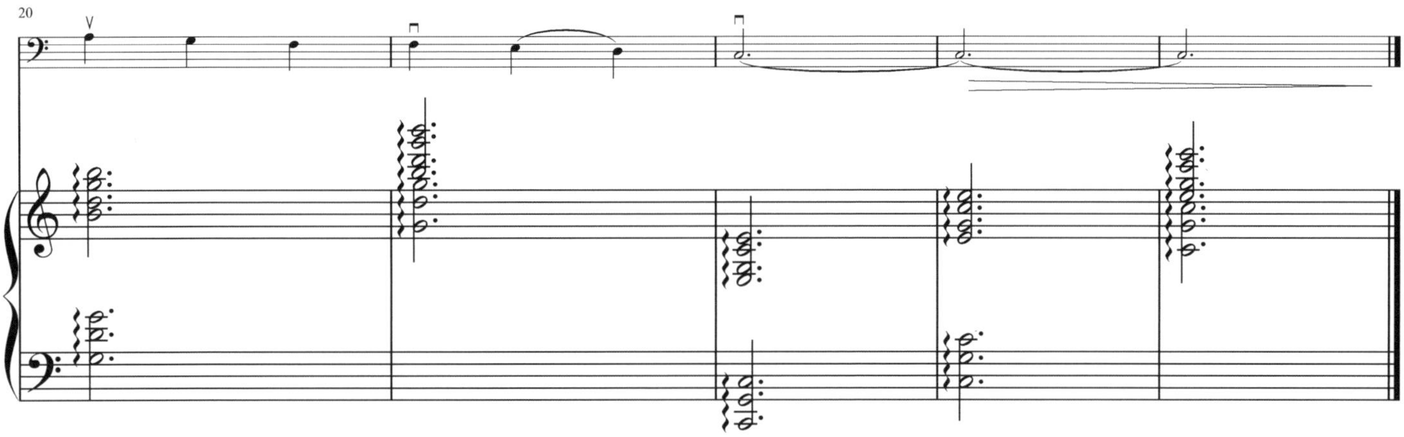

Come and Dance With Me

Christine Watts
Craig Levesque

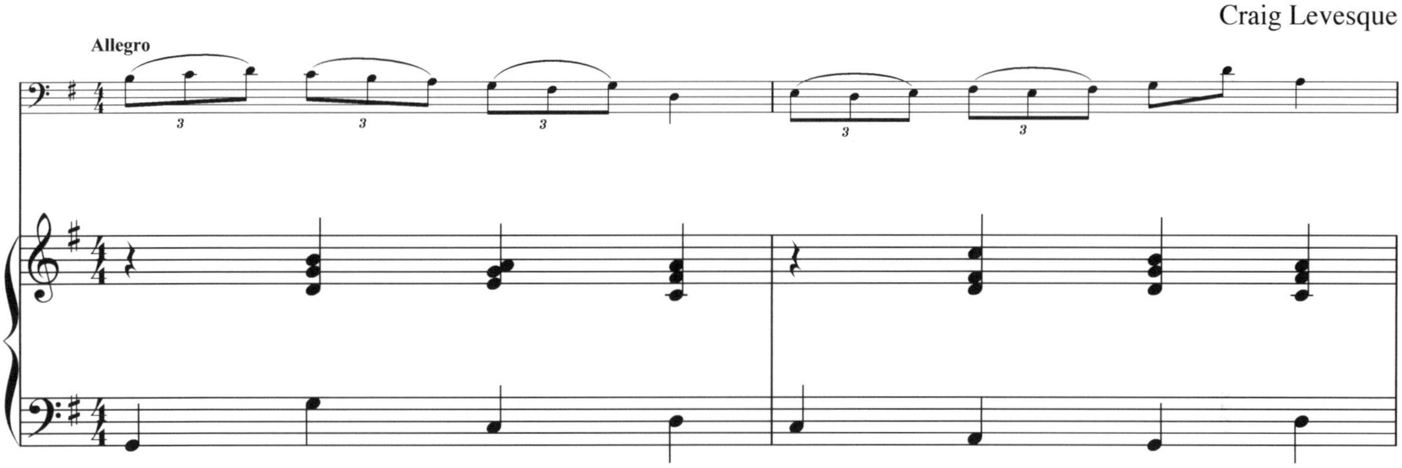

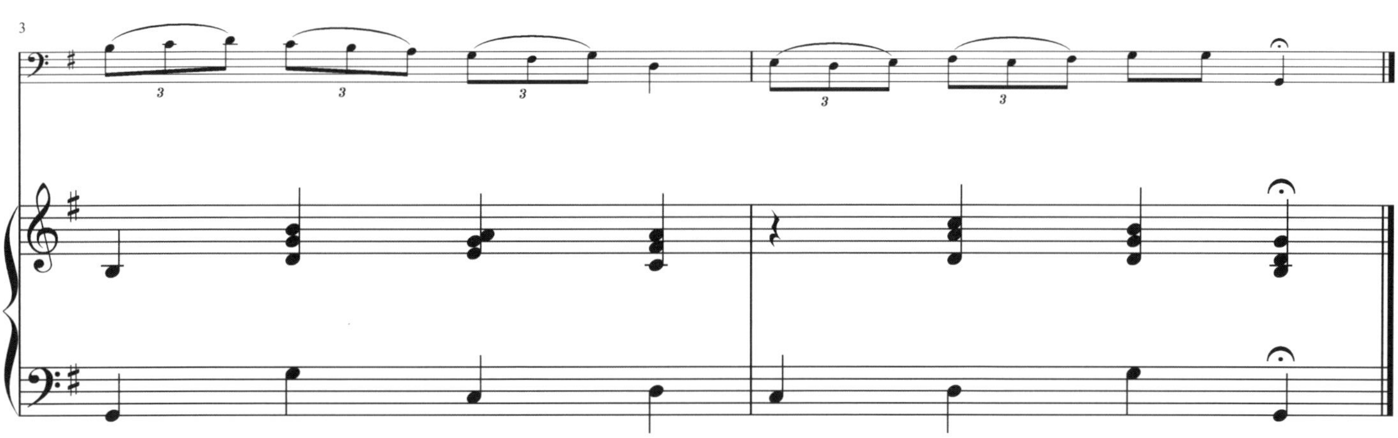

German Dance

Joseph Haydn
Craig Levesque

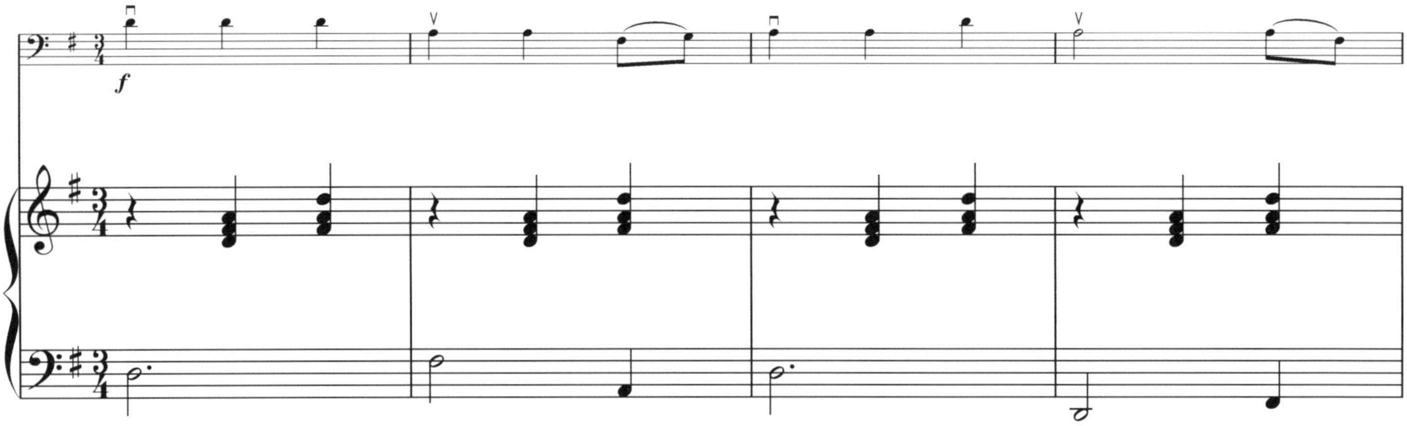

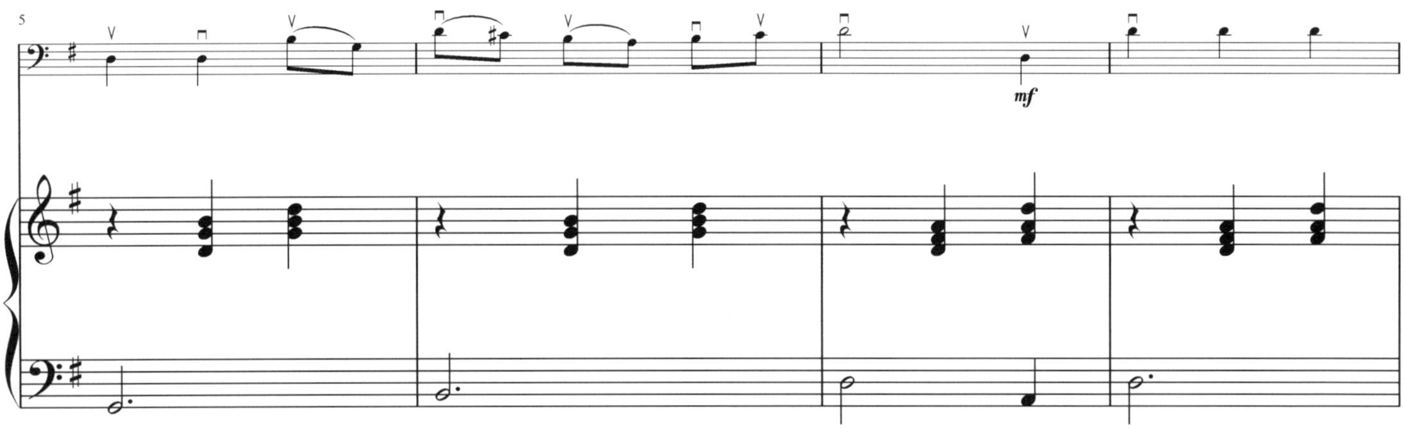

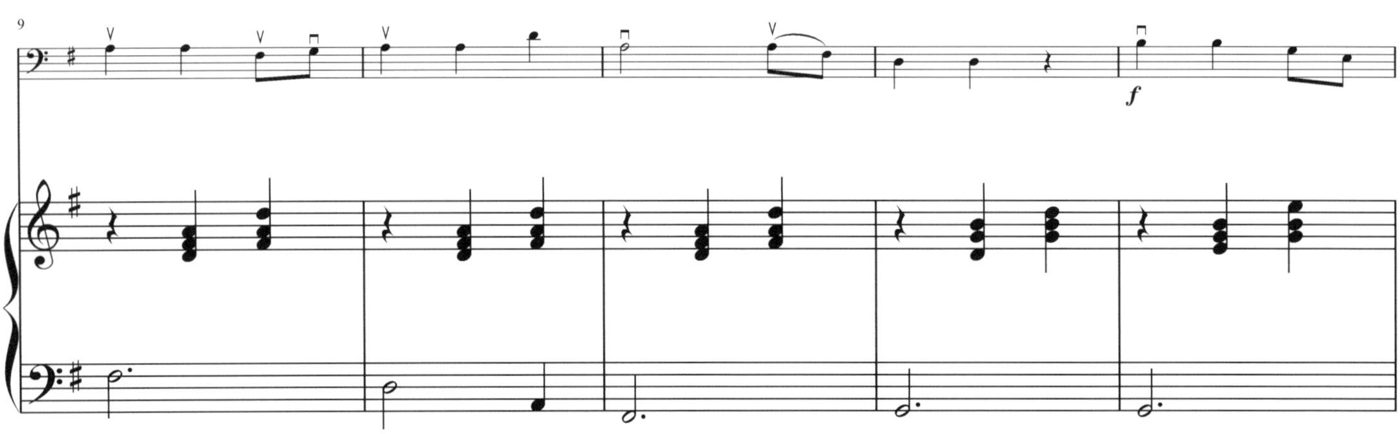

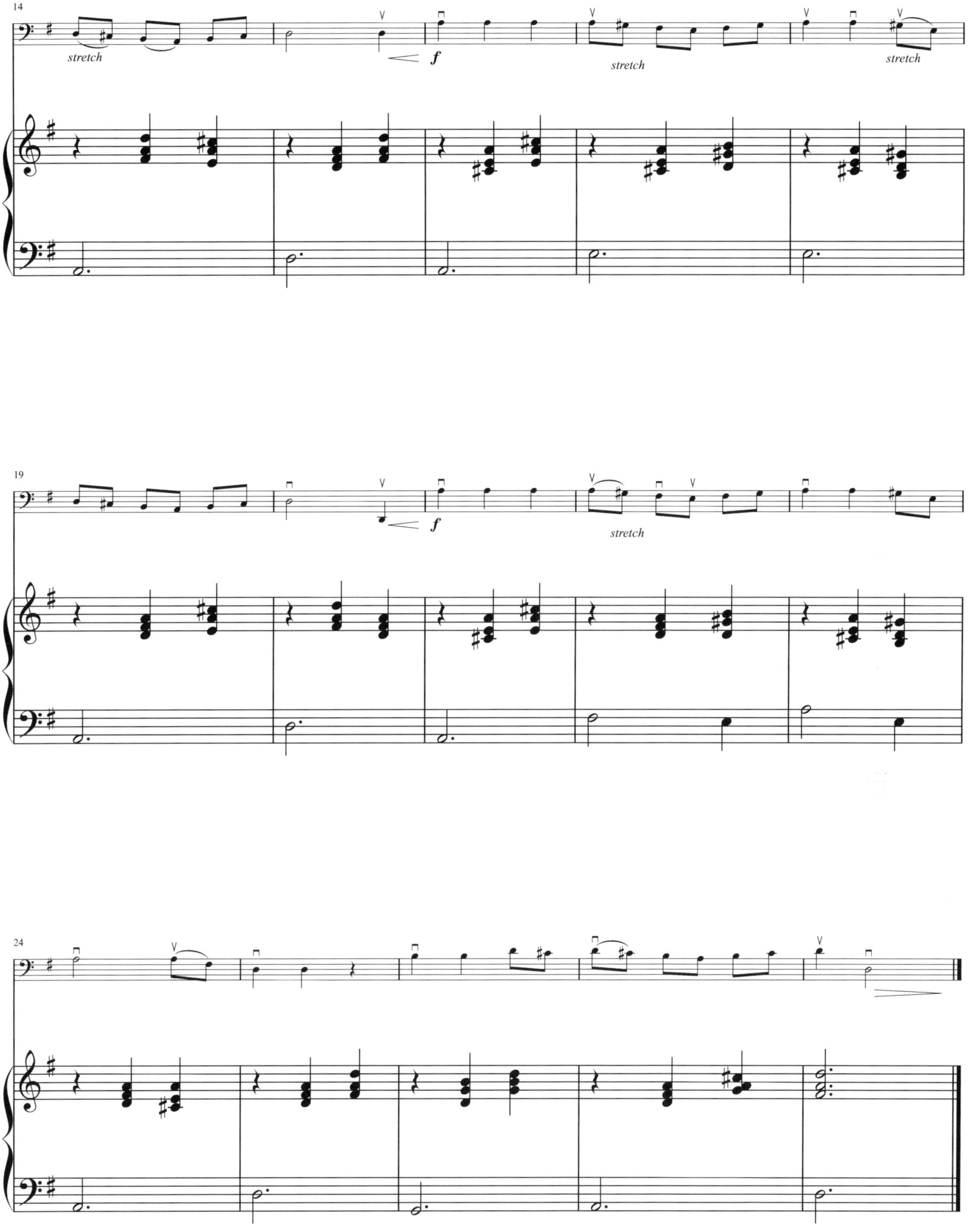
14
stretch
f
stretch
stretch
19
f
stretch
24

Song of Thanksgiving

Edward Kremser
Craig Levesque

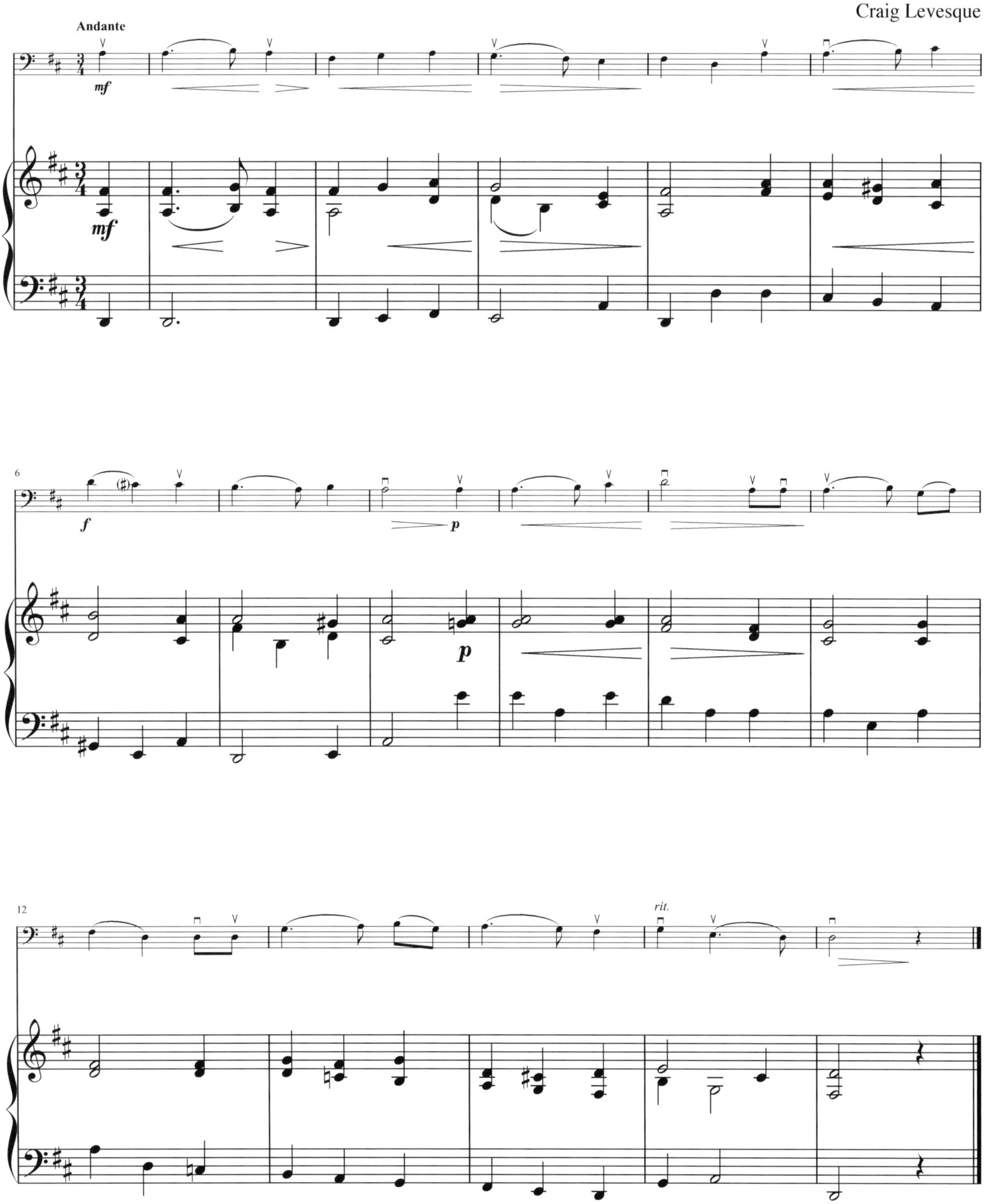

The Three Horsemen

German Folk Song
Craig Levesque

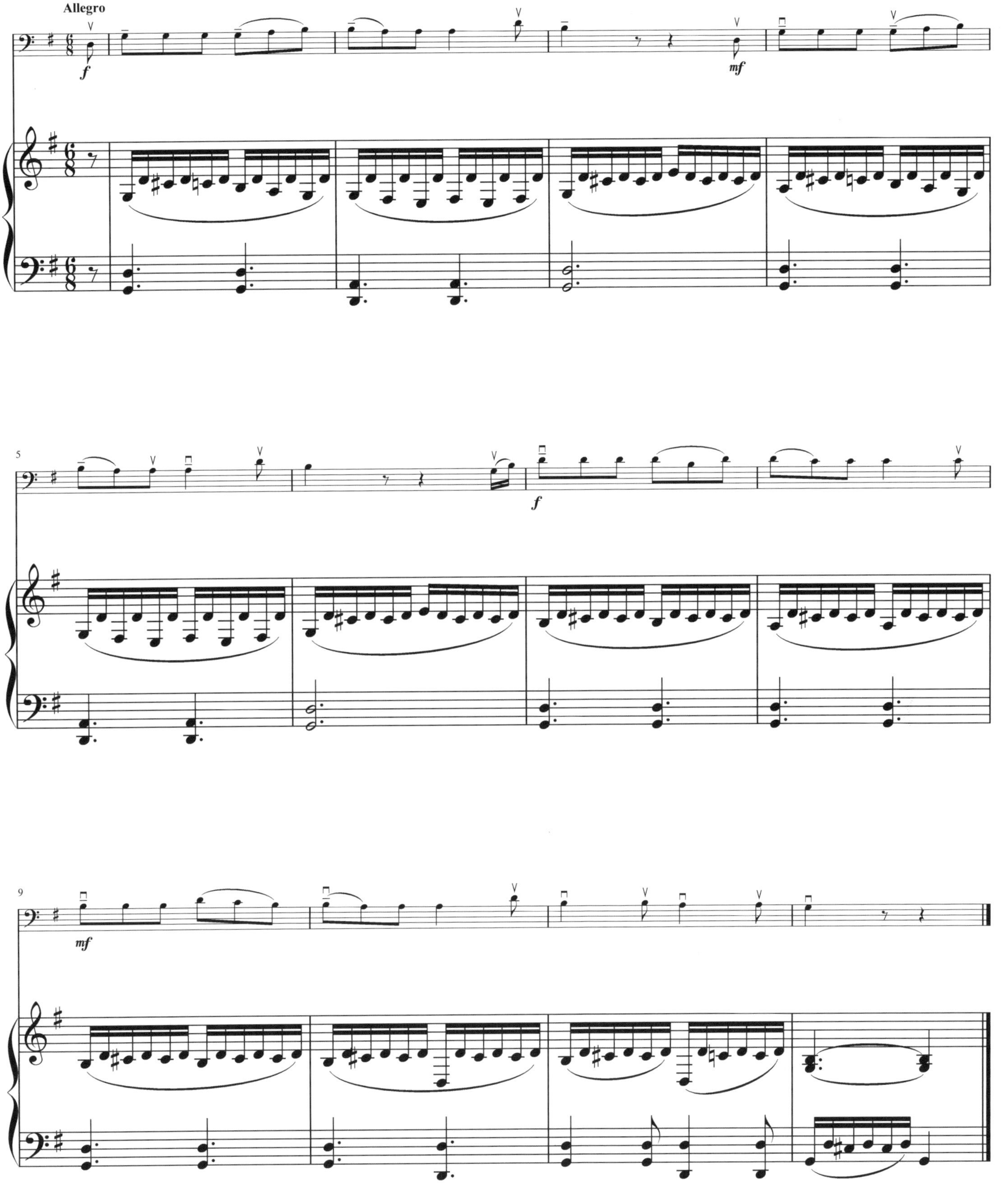

Little Flower

Christine Watts
Sarah Dubois

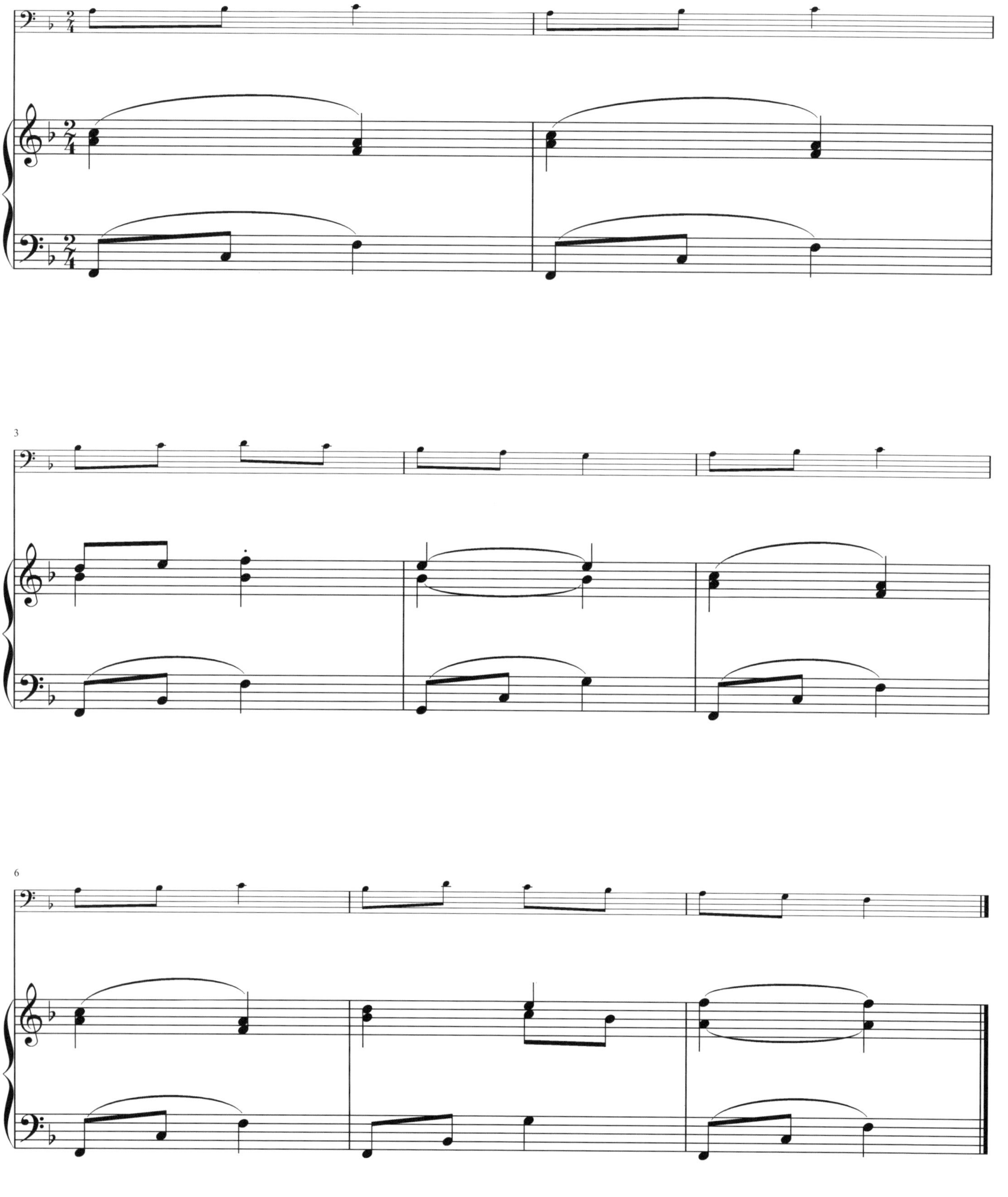

The Cuckoo and the Donkey

C. F. Zelter
Craig Levesque

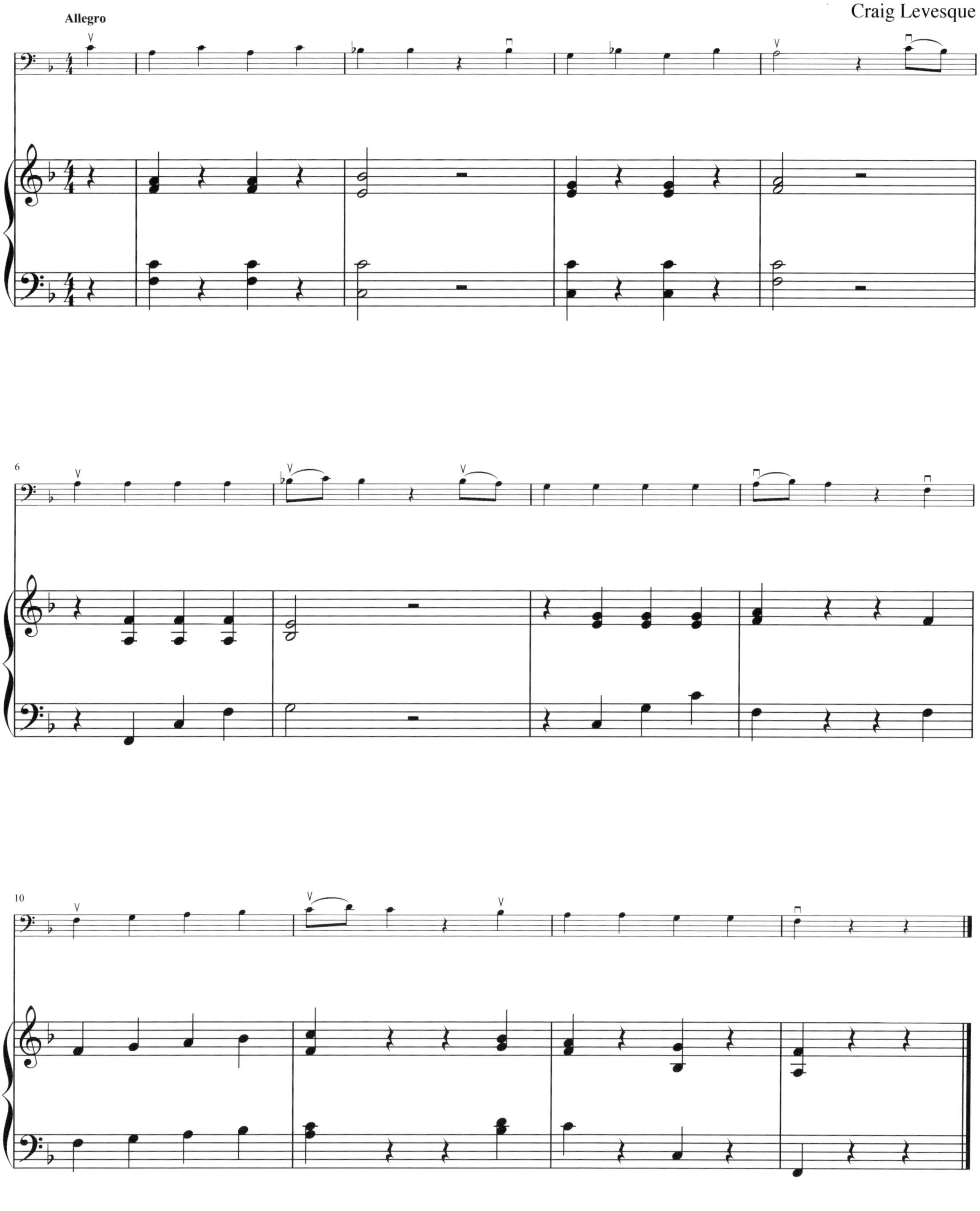

Song of the Sea

Christine Watts
Michi Tashjian

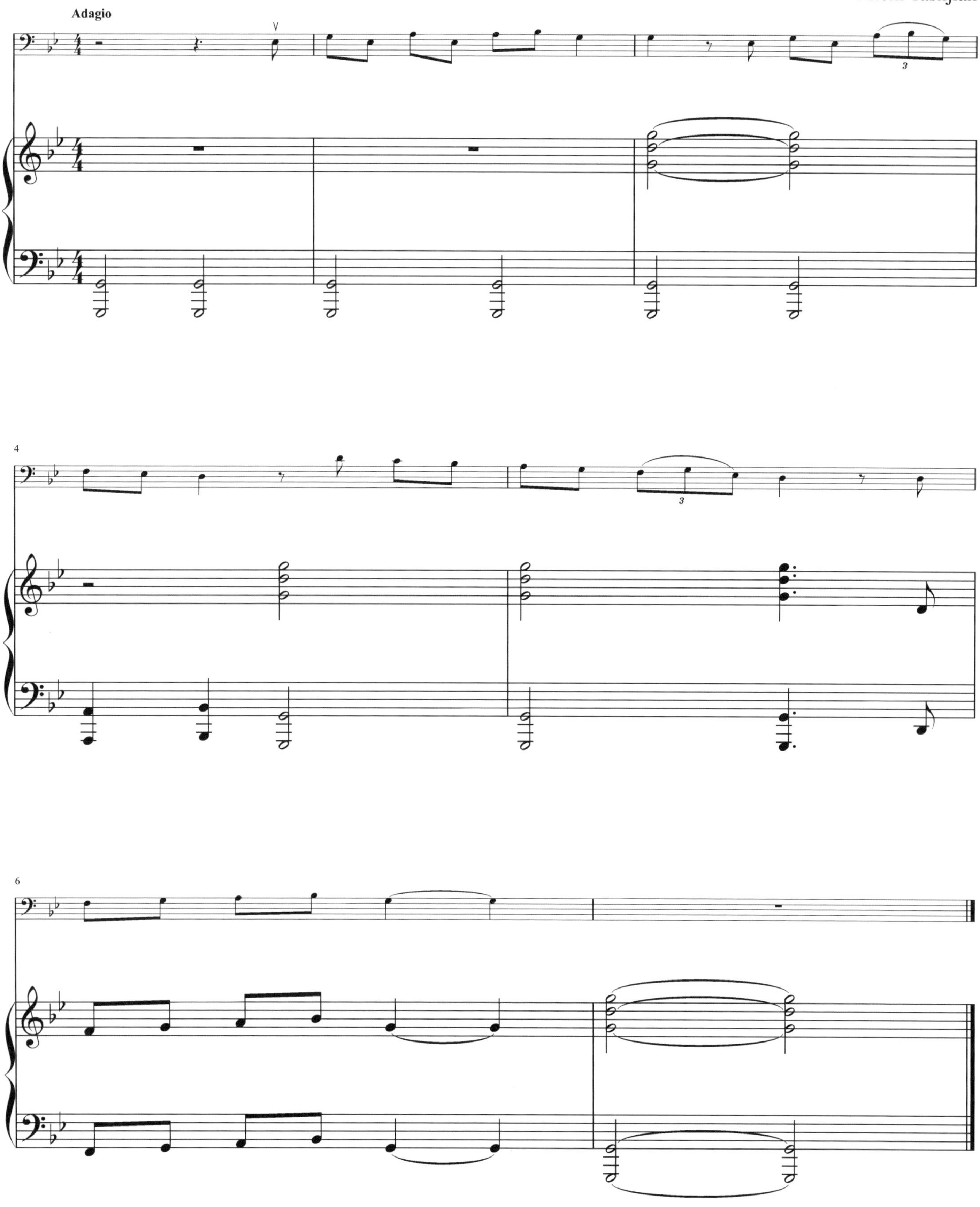

Home on the Range

Brewster Higley and Daniel E. Kelly
Sarah Dubois

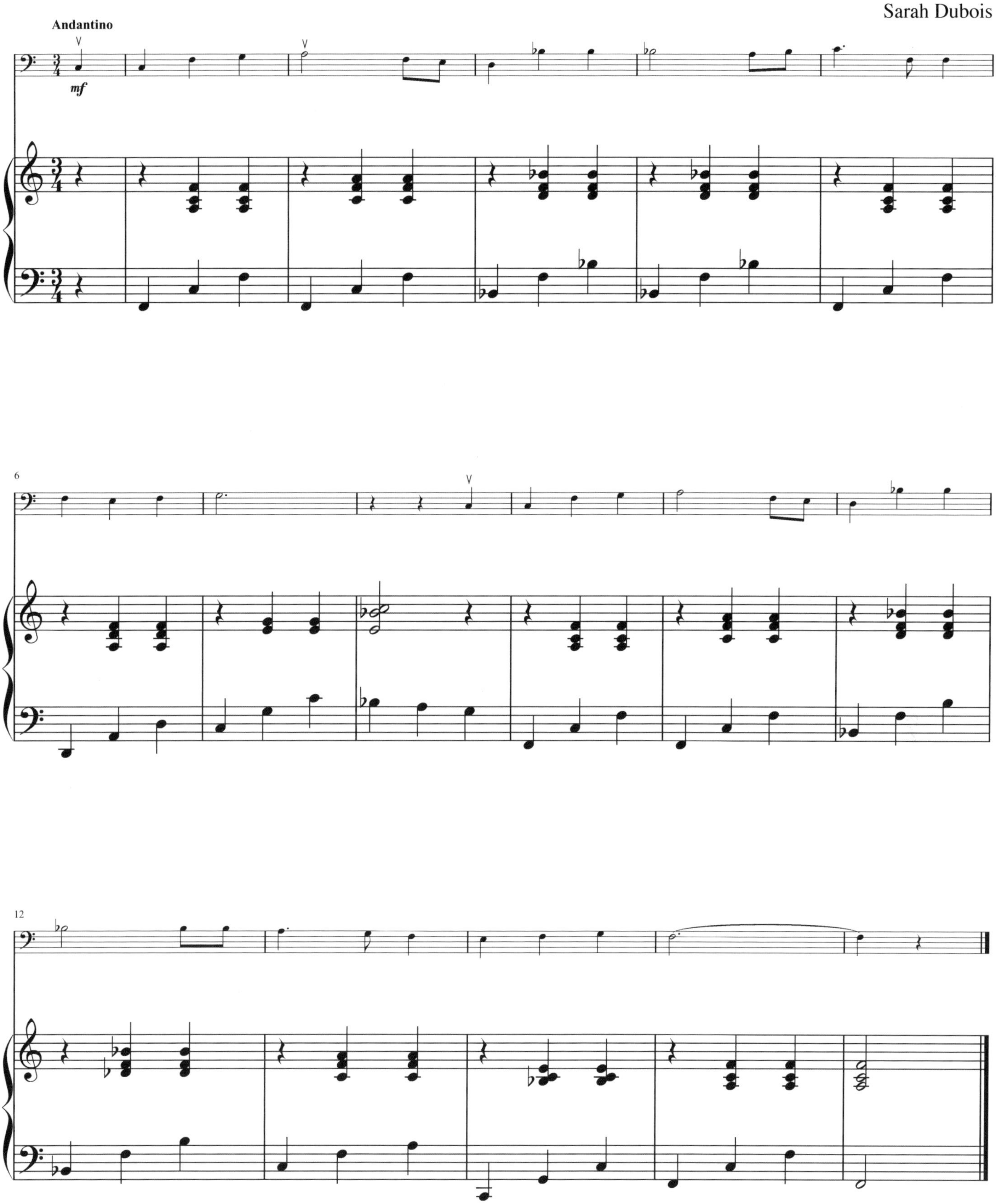

The Wind

Christine Watts
Sarah Dubois

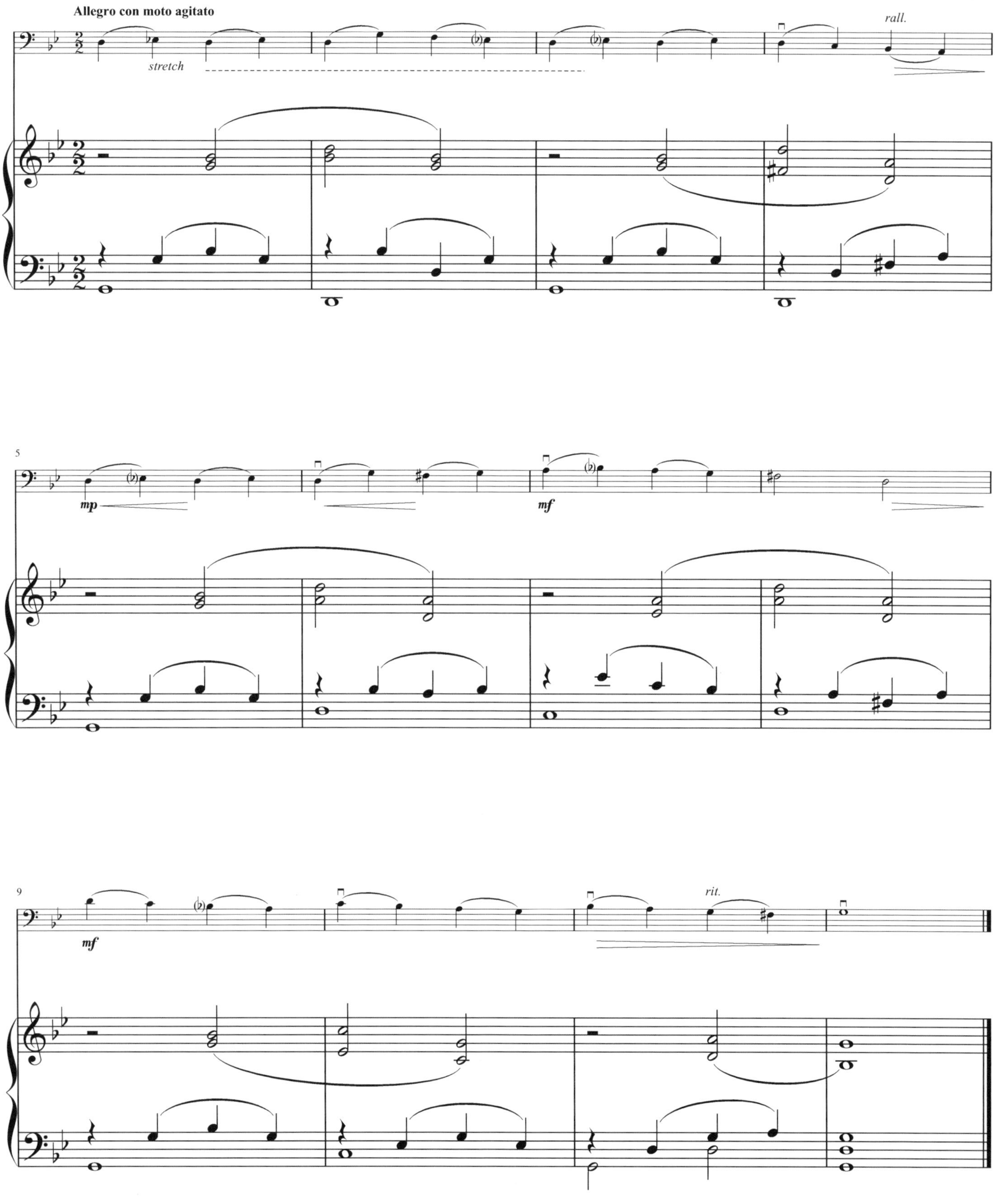

The Nut Tree

Old English Song
Craig Levesque

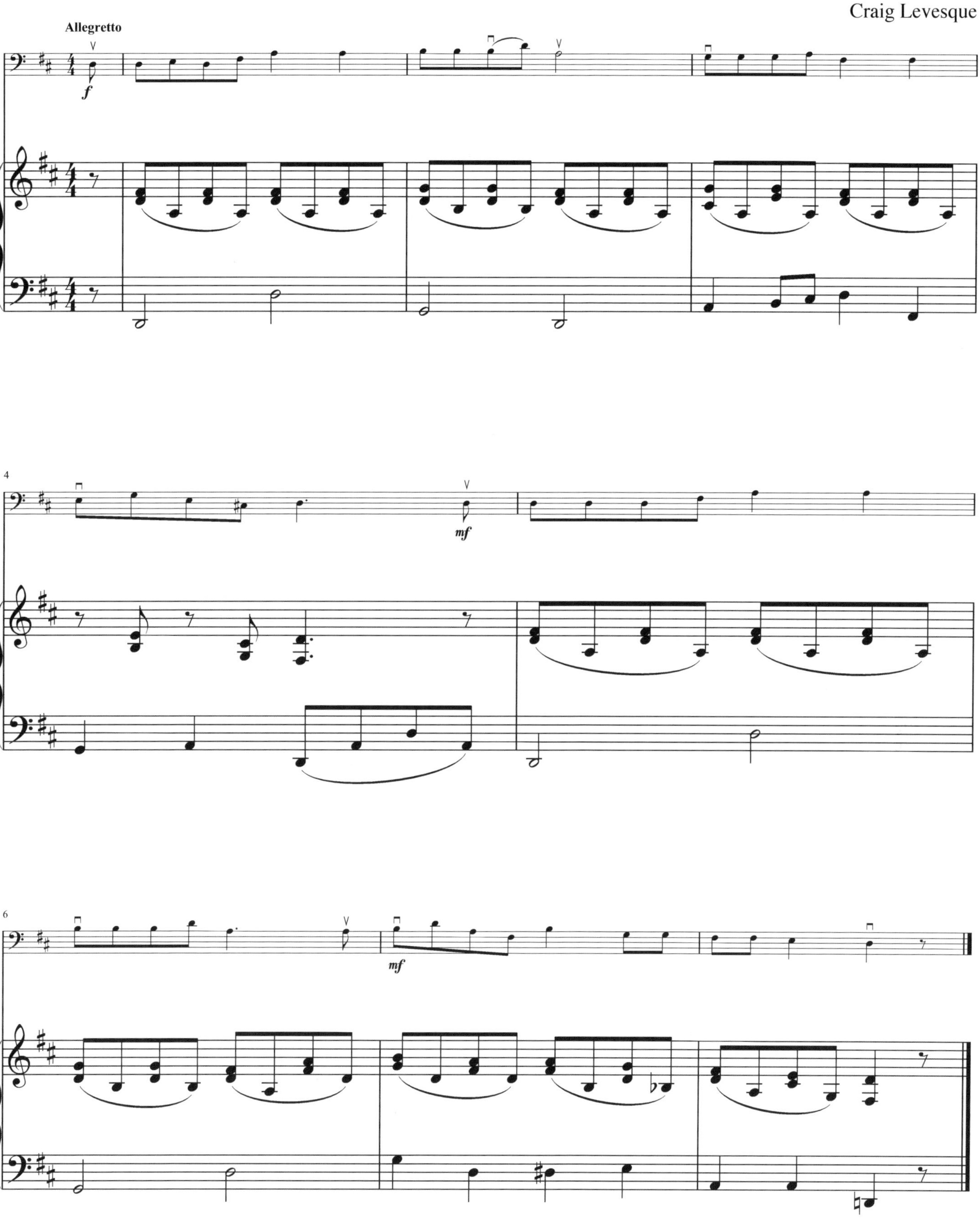

French Folk Song

Folk Song
Sarah Dubois

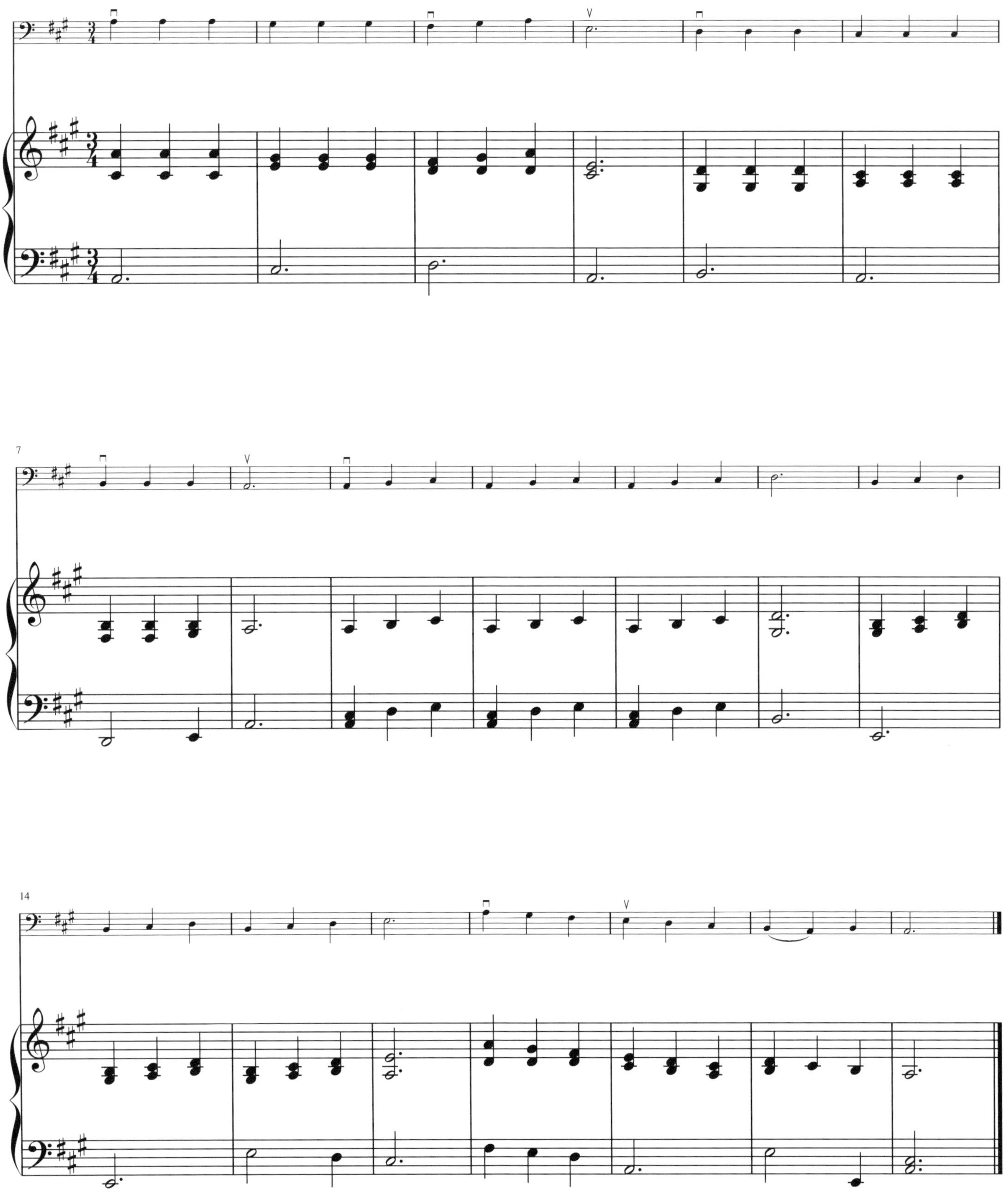

Hop, Hop, Hop

Traditional American
Craig Levesque

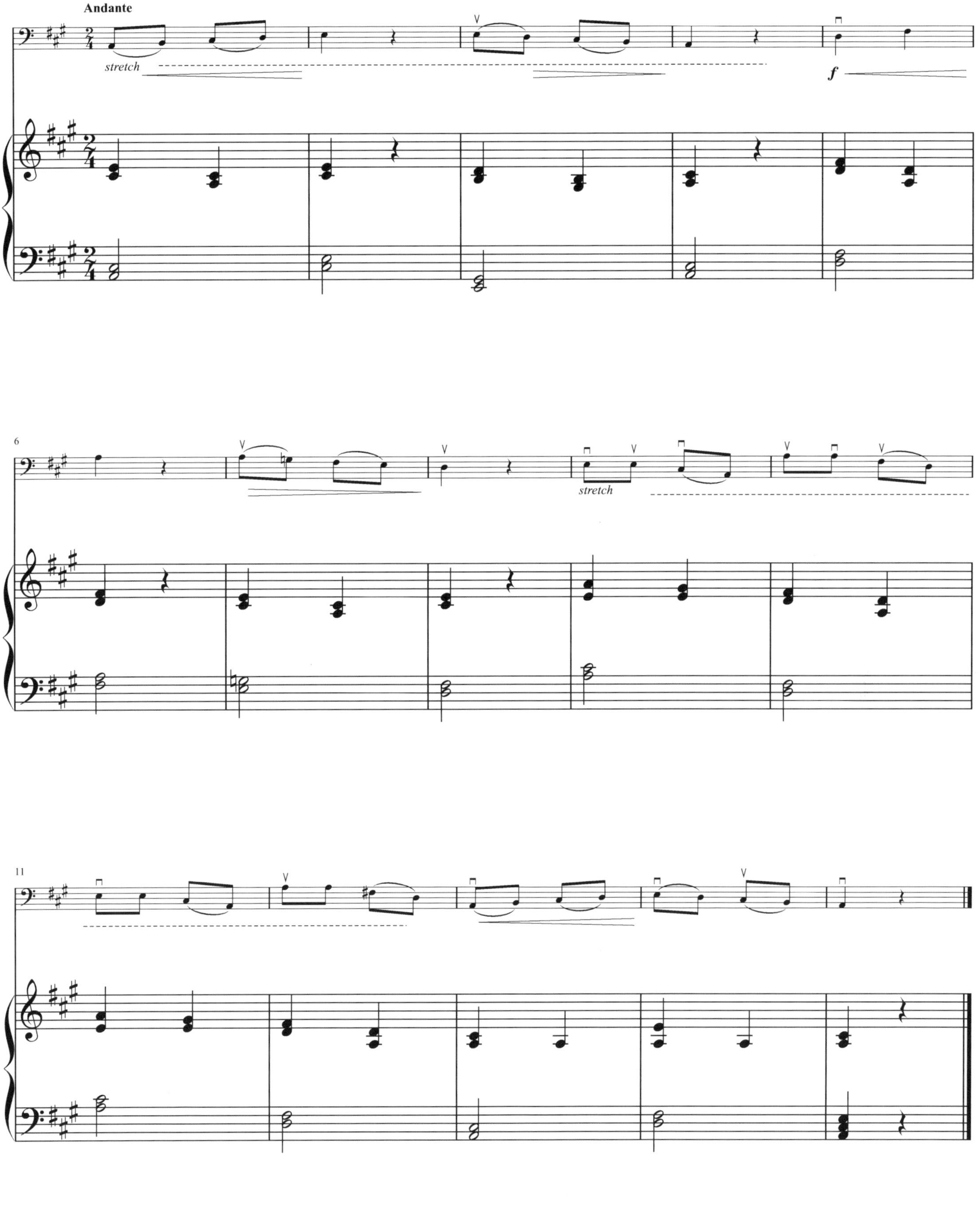

This page has been left blank
to avoid awkward page turns.

Sweet Betsy from Pike

American Folk Song
Sarah Dubois

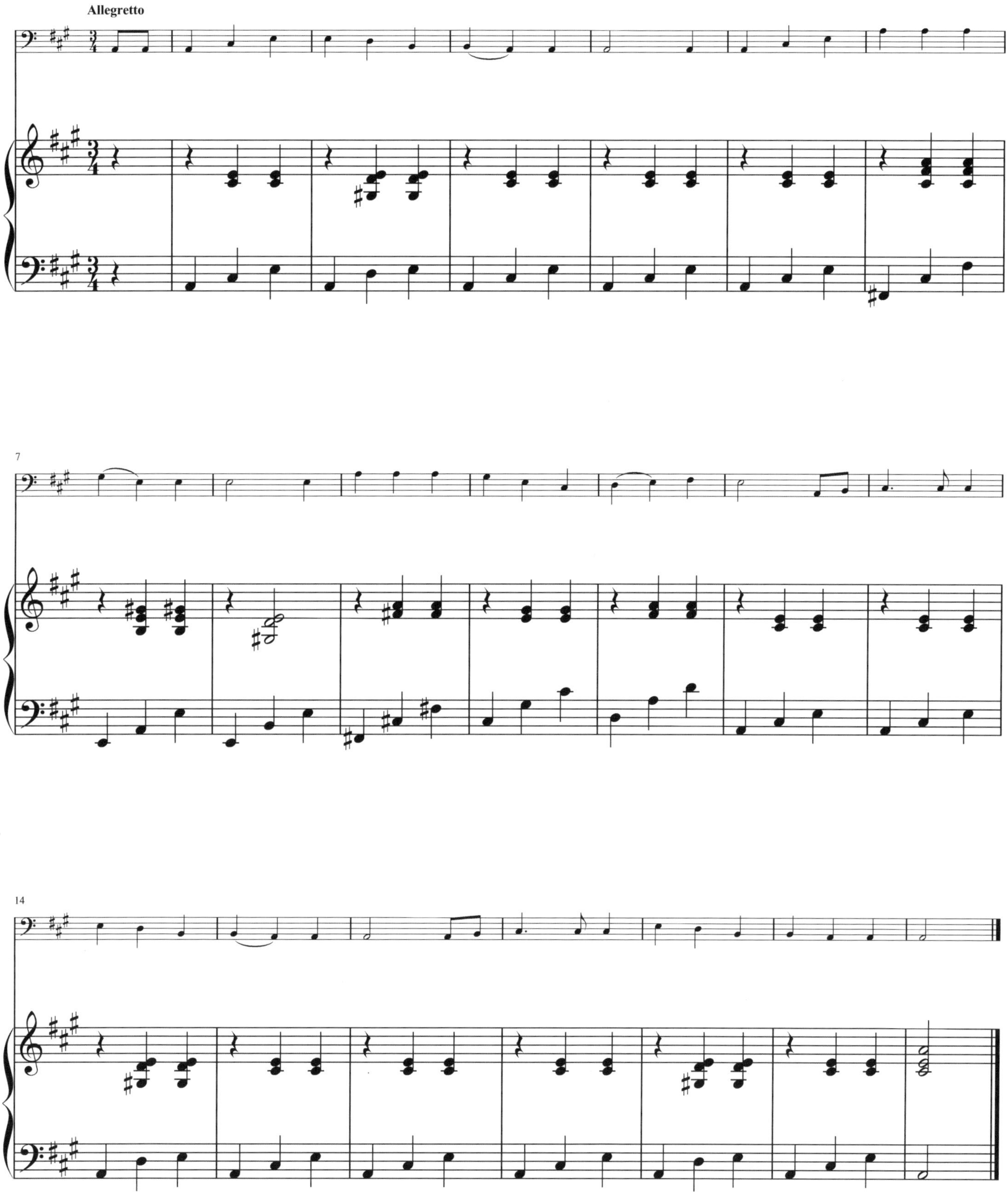

The Dancing Gazelle

Johann Kirnberger
Joseph Kenney

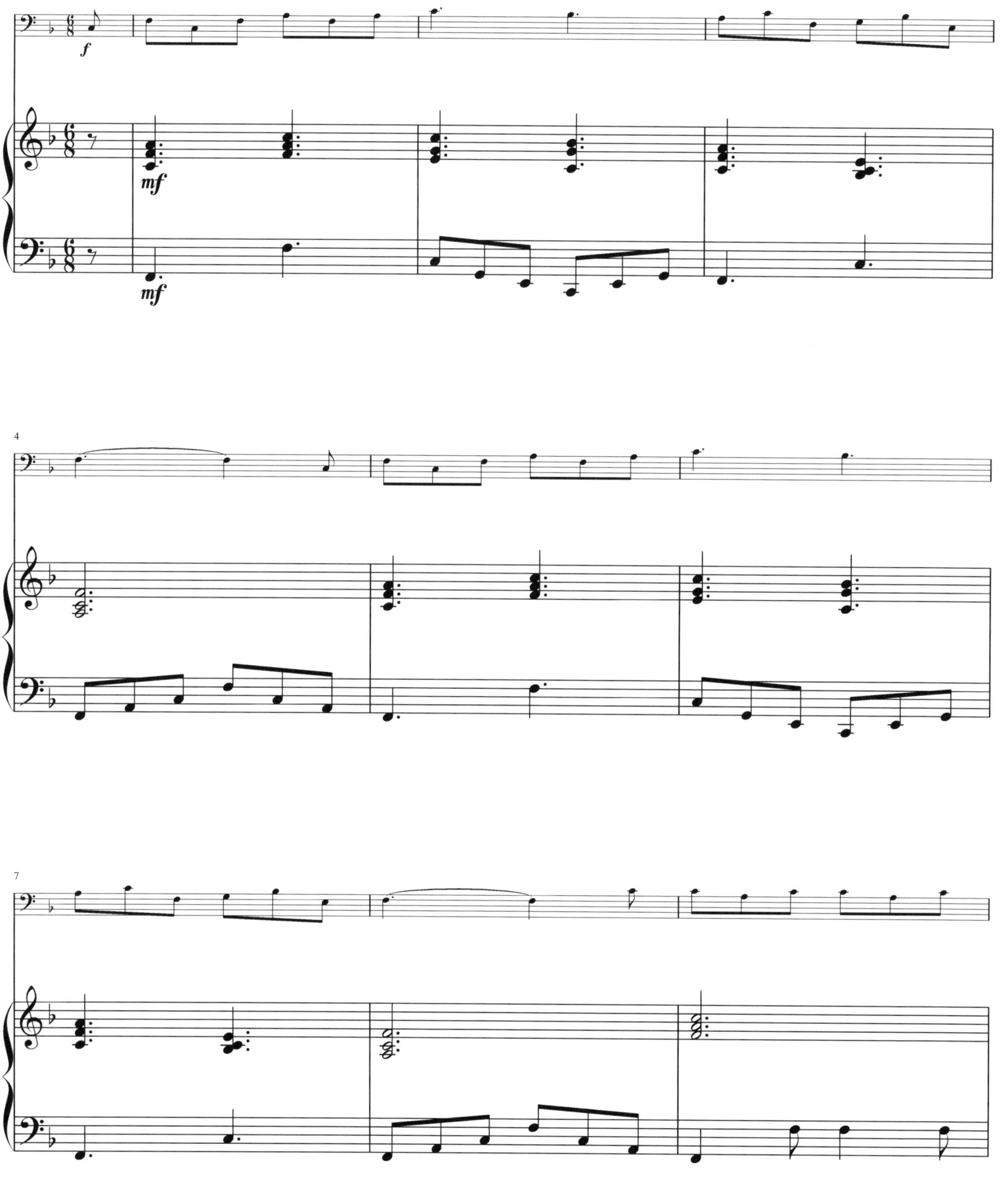

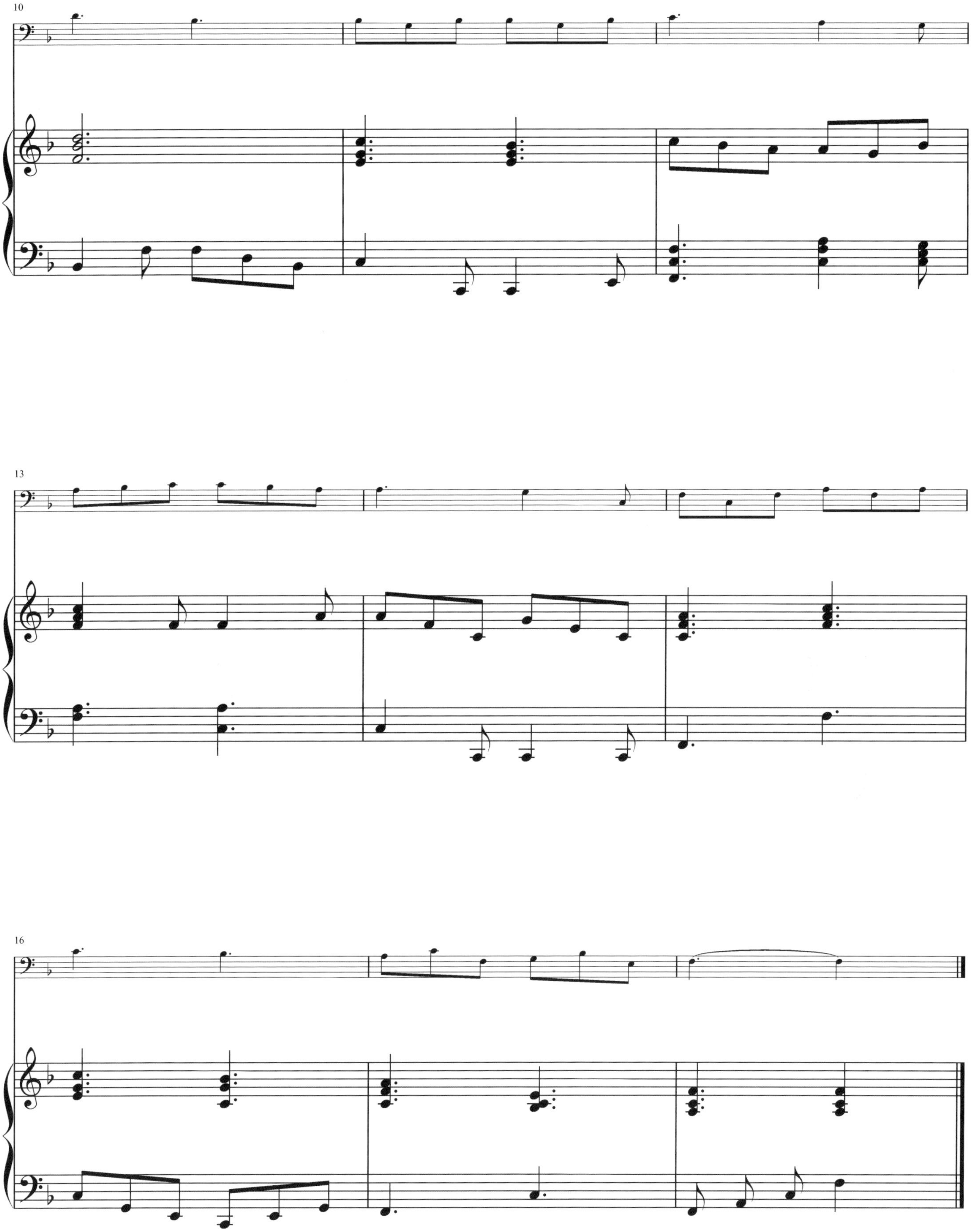
10
13
16

The Graceful Giraffe

17th Century Dance
Craig Levesque

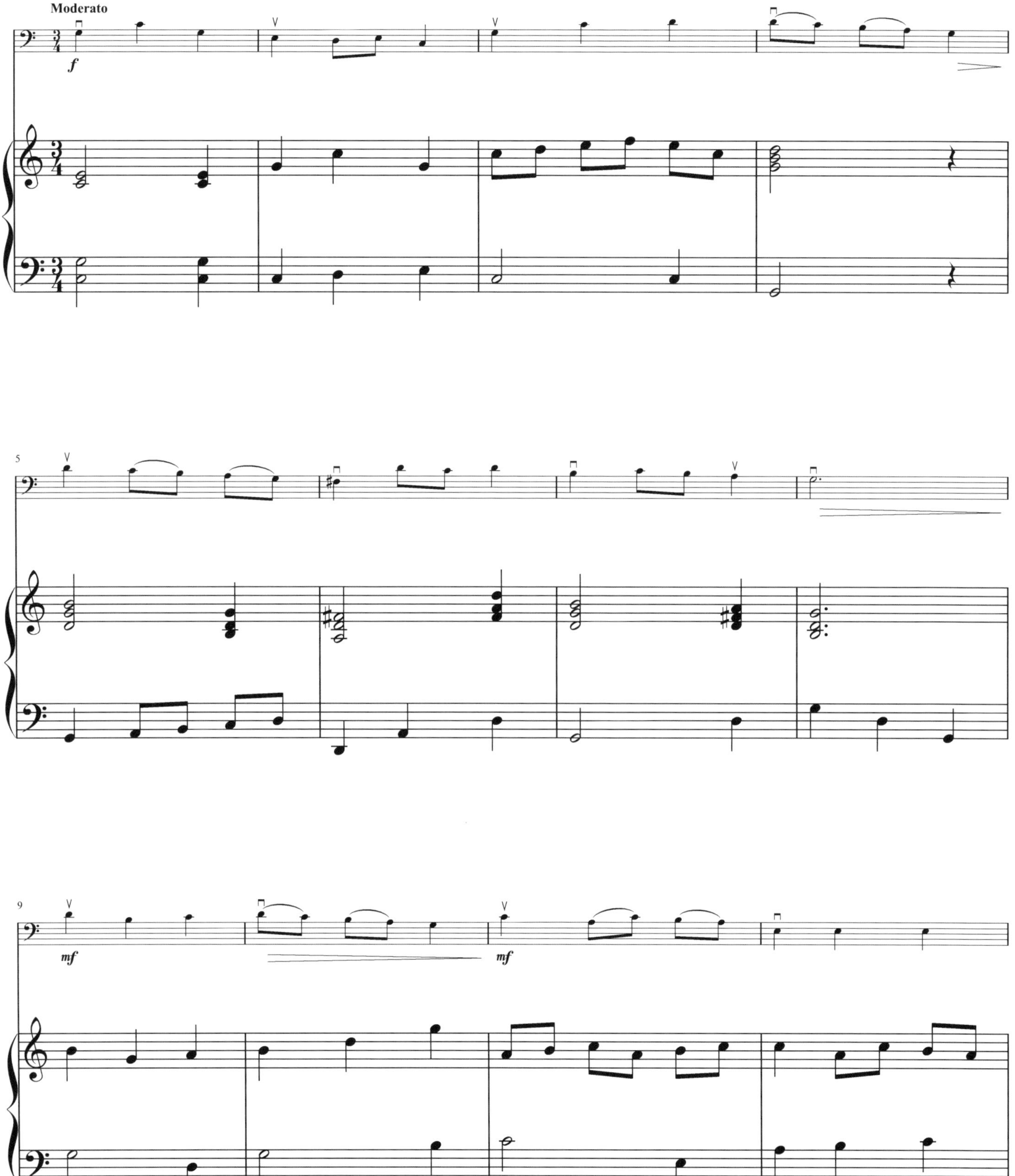

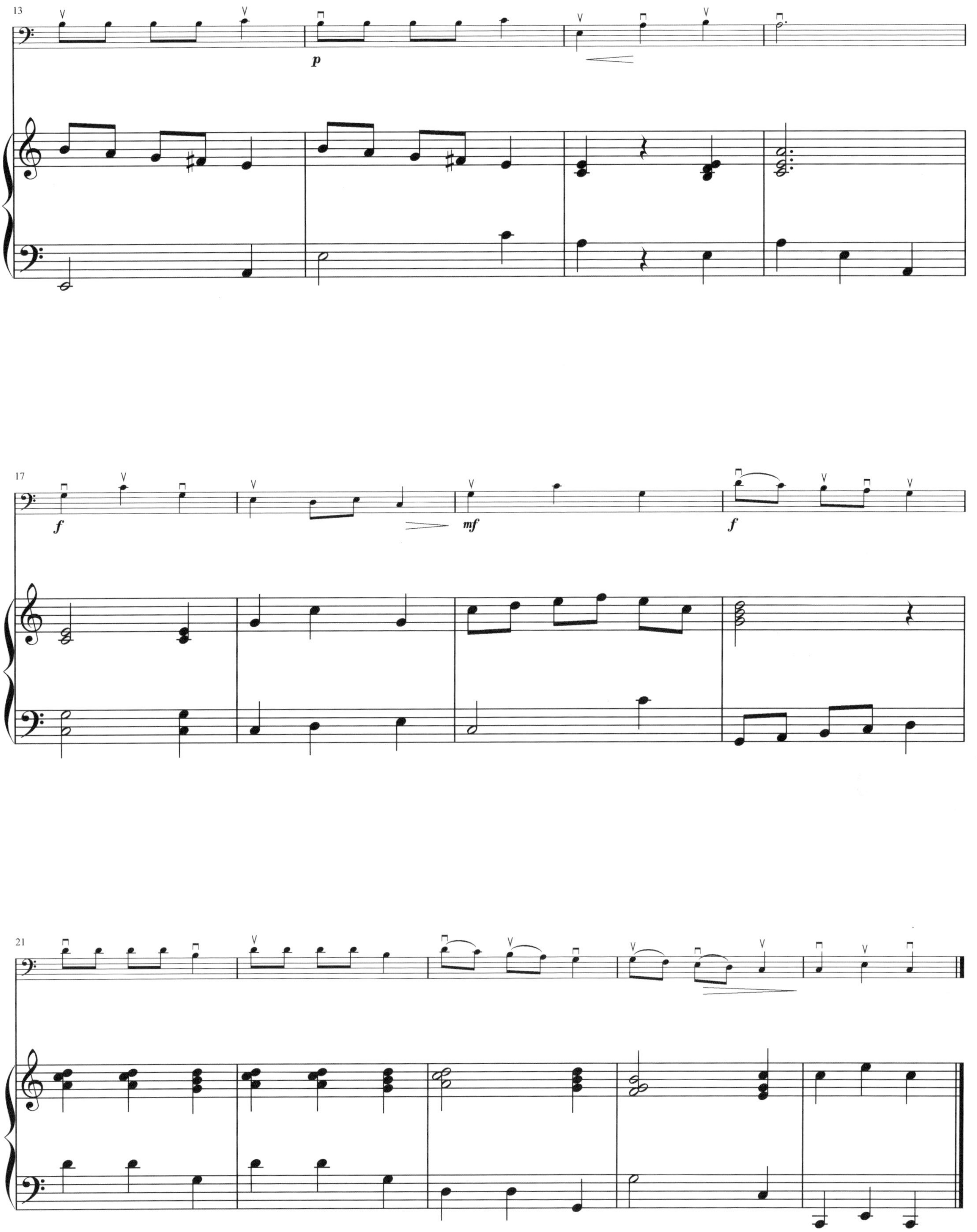
13
p
17
f
mf
f
21

The Jumping Jackrabbit

Daniel Turk
Joseph Kenney

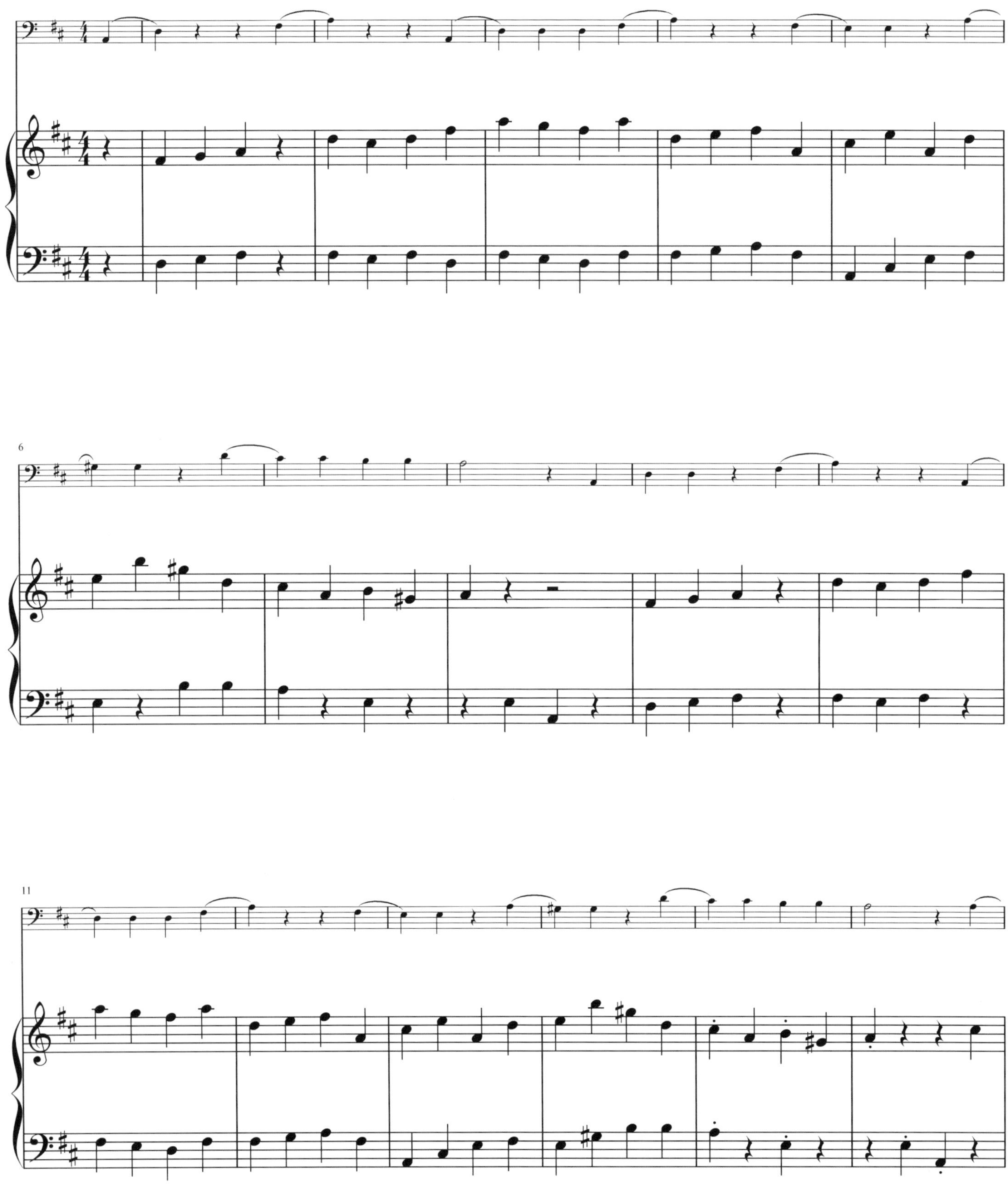

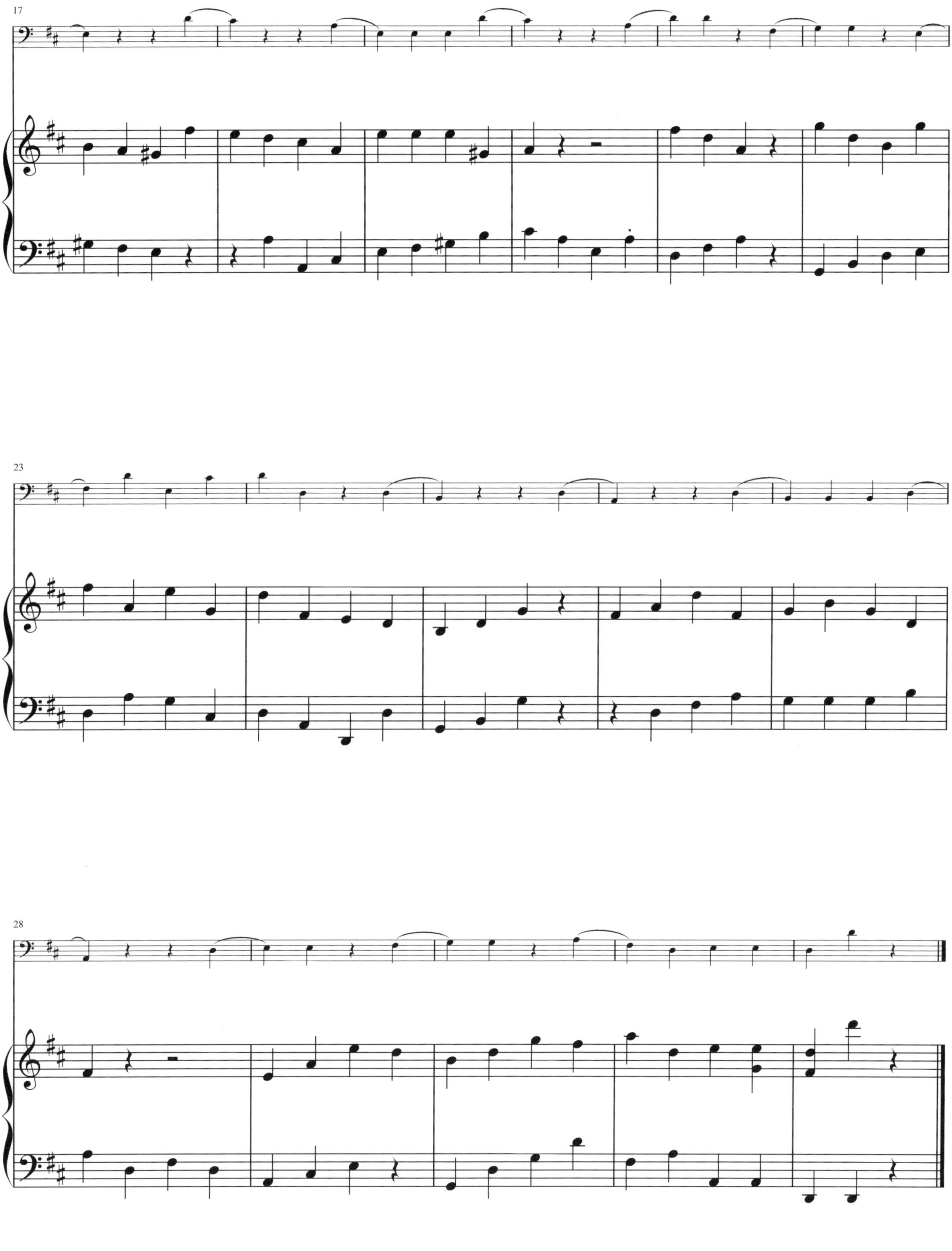
17
23
28

King of the Forest

Christine Watts
Joseph Kenney

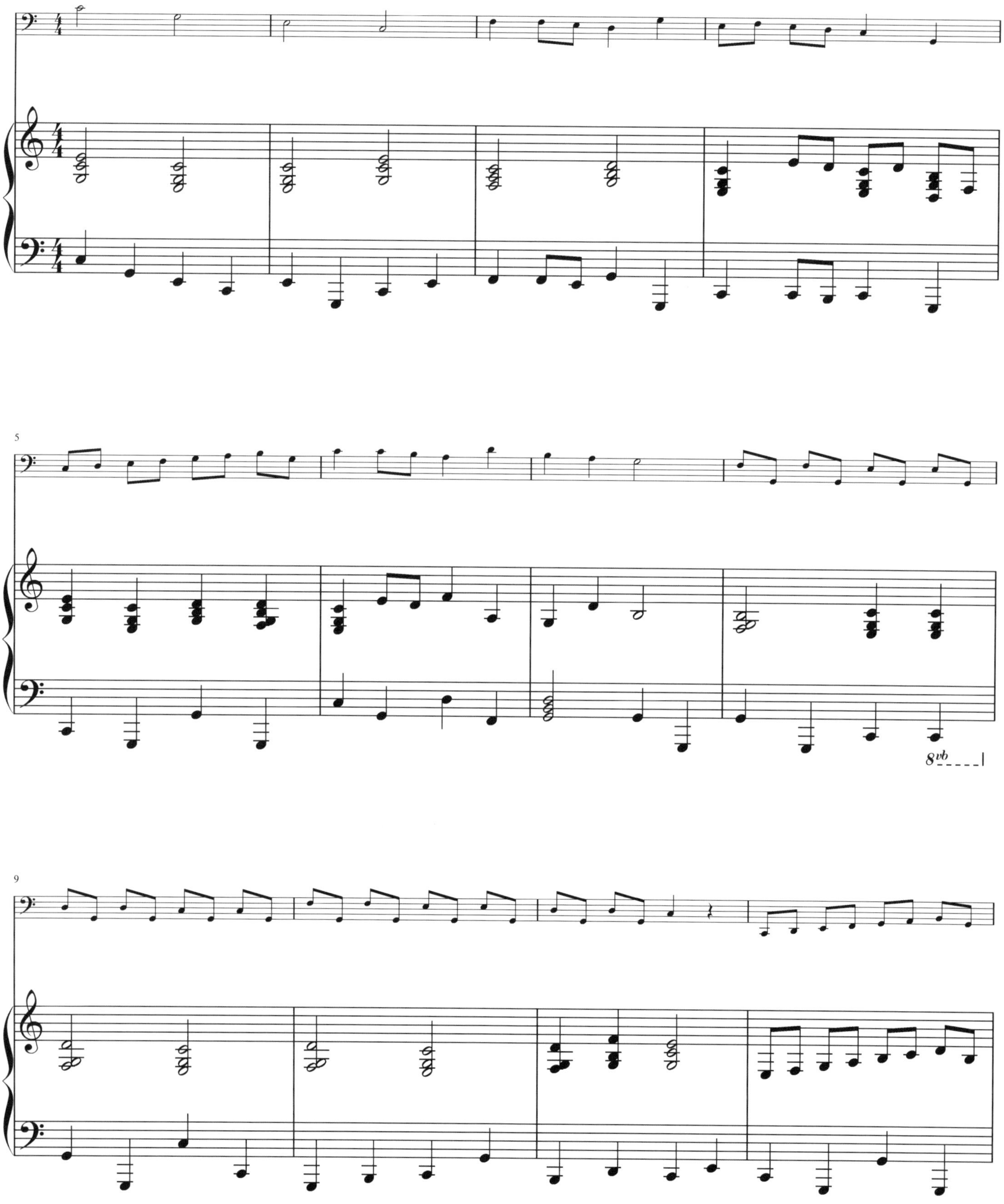

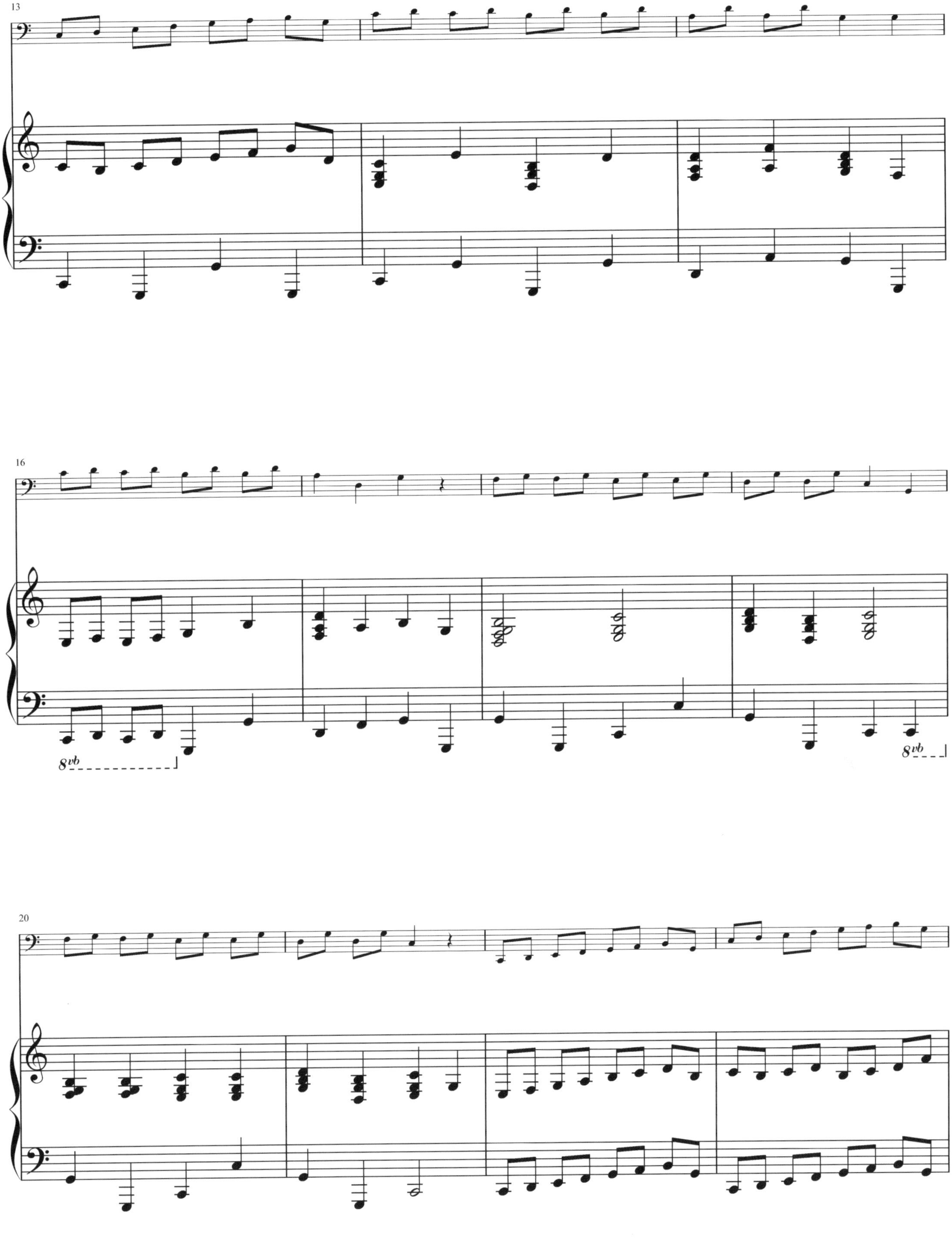
13
16
8vb
8vb
20

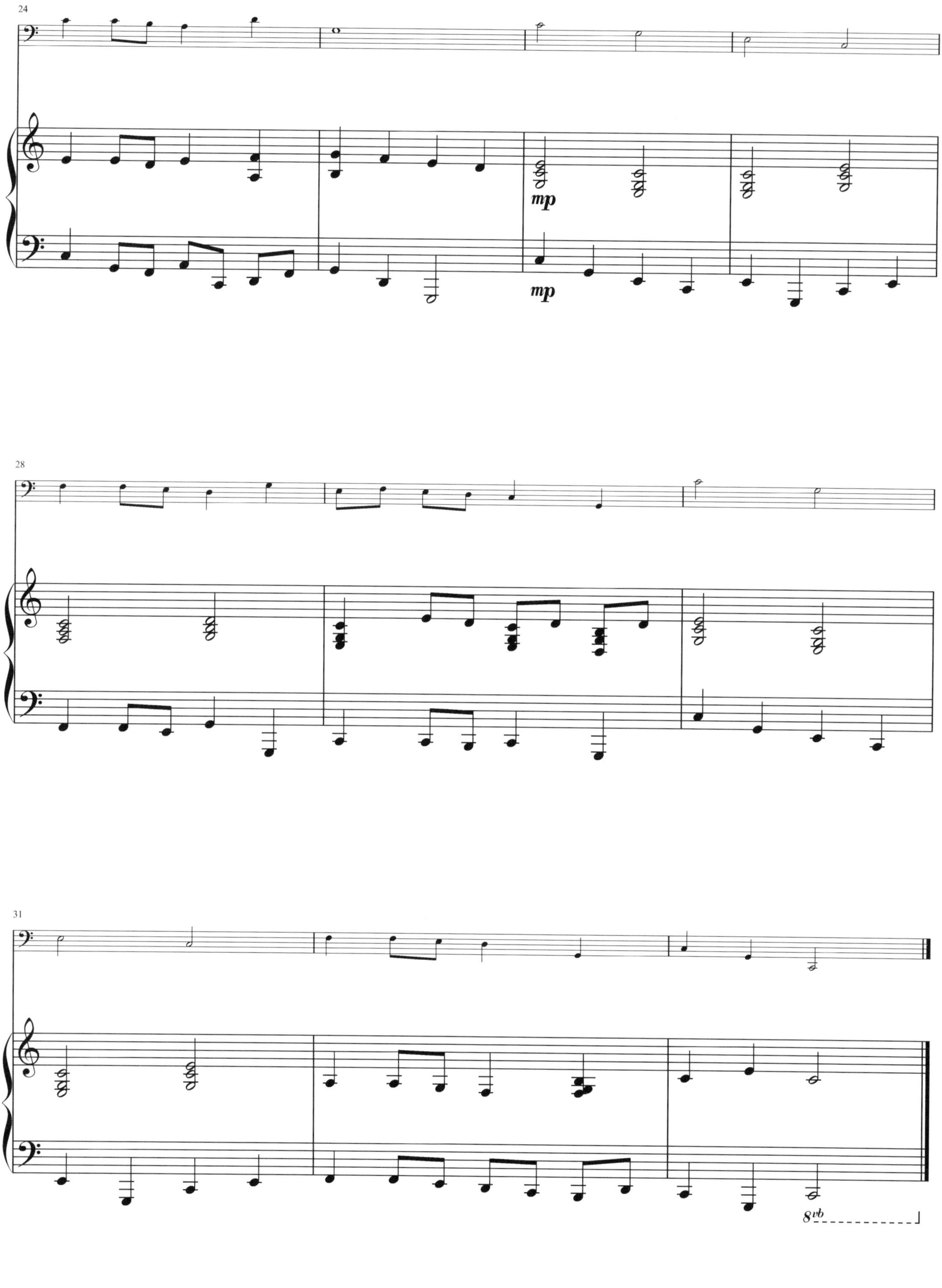
24
mp
mp
28
31
8vb